BY

David S. Broder

Bob Woodward

SIMON & SCHUSTER

New York   London   Toronto   Sydney   Tokyo   Singapore

The Man
Who
Would Be
President
Dan Quayle

SIMON & SCHUSTER
Simon & Schuster Building
Rockefeller Center
1230 Avenue of the Americas
New York, New York 10020

SIMON & SCHUSTER and colophon are registered trademarks
of Simon & Schuster Inc.
Designed by Levavi & Levavi
Manufactured in the United States of America

3   5   7   9   10   8   6   4   2

Library of Congress Cataloging-in-Publication Data
Broder, David S.
The man who would be president   Dan Quayle /
David S. Broder and Bob Woodward.
p.   cm.
1.Quayle, Dan, 1947–   2.Vice-Presidents—United States—
Biography.   I. Woodward, Bob.
II. Quayle, Dan, 1947–   .   III. Title.
E840.8.Q28B76 1992
973.928'092—dc20
[B]   92-8183
                                                  CIP
ISBN: 0-671-79183-4

The contents of this work, excluding the introduction, were
previously published in *The Washington Post.*

CONTENTS

Introduction   9

1. Dan Quayle: The Premeditated Surprise   13

2. The Roots of a Route to Washington—
   1976–1980   31

3. "Control Freak Loses Control"—1988   53

4. Quayle's Reputation vs. the Record   75

5. Facing Limitations in an "Awkward Job"   87

6. The Vice President's Driving Passion   107

7. Quayles and Bushes, Almost Like Family   117

8/10/92

18,00

BeT

7

8. The Competitiveness Council: Curbing
   Federal Rules, Leaving "No Fingerprints"   123

9. The Space Council: Debating NASA's Future   143

10. Marilyn Quayle: Guardian of the
    Quayle Image   153

11. What If Dan Quayle Were to Become
    President?   175

12. Waiting in the Wings for 1996   197

INTRODUCTION

A vice president can become president in an instant. "In case of the removal of the President from office or of his death or resignation, the Vice President shall become President," states the 25th amendment to the U.S. Constitution. No one has to vote, meet or wait. The Constitution requires only that the vice president take the 35-word oath before assuming the duties of president.

Eight presidents in this country's history have died in office, and one, Richard Nixon, resigned. That is one very good reason to take Vice President Dan Quayle seriously.

A relatively obscure senator when he burst into prominence as Bush's surprise running mate in August 1988, Quayle has been examined almost exclusively in a hothouse or crisis atmosphere. Whether immediately after Bush's selection of Quayle, or during President Bush's two health scares, journalists have had to scramble to evaluate the man who might suddenly become the chief executive. Each time it became clear that no one knew enough about him. A few days of frantic reporting was not sufficient to understand the man.

Over the last three years, serious assessments of Quayle have taken a back seat to jokes about him. In part because of his unimpressive and gaffe-ridden performance during the 1988 presidential campaign, Quayle has been saddled with a reputation as a lightweight and treated as a figure of fun. The news media have generally taken notice of him only when he has done something to live up to his image as a boyish buffoon. So the real Dan Quayle remains largely unknown.

The office Quayle holds has also been misunderstood, ignored or ridiculed. Few bother to make the effort to understand what the vice presidency is or how it works. The office is one of the black holes of American journalism.

Unlike the secretaries of state, defense or the treasury, the vice president controls no clearly defined territory. Yet since Walter Mondale assumed the office in 1977, vice presidents have gained importance and responsibility in the inner councils of the White House. Once relegated to the outer reaches of an administration, the vice president is now as close as anyone to the center of power. For this reason, the office warrants greater scrutiny than it has received.

In mid-1991 *The Washington Post* decided to look behind the caricature of Dan Quayle to try to learn more about the man and the office. We spent six months preparing for the *Post* a long series of articles on Quayle, which ran from January 5 to 12, 1992, and are reprinted in this book. We interviewed more than 200 present and former colleagues and opponents, critics and friends. We had four lengthy conversations with his wife, Marilyn Tucker Quayle, and twenty formal interviews with Vice President Quayle between June and November 1991. Quayle cooperated with our inquiry, enabling us to see his activities at close range, to speak at length with his associates, and to ask any question that we found important. In these articles, we tried to offer the most comprehensive account of a sitting vice president ever written.

The 1992 political campaign has rekindled the debate over the responsibility the news media has for the quality of information that is available for political discussion in this country. Not only campaign coverage, but the daily presentation of political issues and politicians should rise above the lowest common denominator established by quick, drive-by journalism, sometimes fed by the latest allegation from the supermarket tabloids or gossip columns. The press should try to elevate the level of discussion, focusing on substantive questions of policy, ideas and the day-to-day workings of government. This endeavor should also include presenting fuller, more definitive portraits of public officials. We believe this is what voters want.

Four people at *The Washington Post* made this project possible: Leonard Downie, Jr., the executive editor; Robert G. Kaiser, the managing editor; Karen DeYoung, the assistant managing editor for national news, who spent weeks

11

editing the articles and guiding us; and Wendy Ross, the assistant news editor, who laid out the articles and photographs. Special thanks to photographer Ray Lustig, to copyeditors Bill O'Brian, Keith Sinzinger and Tom Lansworth, and to Olwen Price for her excellent work.

David Greenberg provided invaluable assistance to us in the research and reporting, writing and editing of these articles.

DAVID S. BRODER
BOB WOODWARD

February 1992

1. Dan Quayle:
The Premeditated Surprise

FEBRUARY 1988 TO AUGUST 1988

Vice President Bush posing with the Quayles in Washington in 1984. Dan Quayle's parents, James C. and Corinne Quayle, are at left. Working behind the scenes in 1988, Quayle challenged the heavyweights in the Reagan administration and won the notice of George Bush.

O n the day after the February 1988 New Hampshire presidential primary, Dan Quayle, then the 41-year-old junior senator from Indiana, called two top aides into his office. "You know," he said, raising his hand and placing his thumb and forefinger about an eighth of an inch apart, so just a sliver of sunlight could be seen in the gap, "Bob Dole was this close."

Quayle saw an opportunity. Vice President George Bush's 9-percentage-point victory over the Republican senator from Kansas meant Bush was unstoppable in the race for the Republican presidential nomination. And while Dole, as a fellow midwesterner, never would have chosen Quayle as his running mate, Quayle figured that Bush just might.

At that meeting, Quayle said he wanted to launch an unofficial, sub rosa campaign to become Bush's choice for vice president. The effort is one he acknowledges only reluctantly today, and only after he is presented with information provided by others.

"You don't run for vice president," he said in one of 20 interviews conducted between June and November 1991 for these articles. "But let me say that there're ways you can be put on the available chart. And without a lot of fanfare, because . . . when you let people know you're going to do something and you don't achieve it, it's a failure. So you keep expectations down and do things as quietly and subtly as possible."

Quayle knew that even if he were not to emerge as Bush's final choice, a place on the vice presidential short list would mark him as a comer in national politics. "We basically figured it was win-win," recalled Marilyn Quayle, his wife of 19 years and a central player in his political life.

Six months after New Hampshire, when Bush announced at the Republican National Convention in New Orleans that he had picked Quayle as his running mate, it seemed a fluke, a rare moment of political caprice on Bush's part. To much of America, Quayle appeared to have come out of nowhere—an anonymous, boyish baby boomer plucked inexplicably from the rear ranks of 40-something conservative politicians.

But for J. Danforth Quayle, his selection was the happy result of months of subtle, even stealthy planning—a quality not commonly associated with his name.

"People have a misconception of him that he just kind of sits back and lets things happen," said Marilyn Quayle. "He likes to appear that way. But he makes things happen. He nudges it along, so that it'll come out his way. He's always thinking, always figuring. He has a very good understanding of human nature. He knows what buttons to push with most people, what'll work and what won't work."

What the Quayles did not foresee was that sharply negative media and public reaction to his selection for the No. 2 spot, along with his repeated stumbles during the campaign, would create a seemingly indelible image of Quayle as an incompetent, dazed youth thrown in among the grown-ups. During the three years of his vice presidency, his lightweight image has been a staple in the repertoire of comedians and comic-strip satirists. Half the Americans questioned in a series of recent polls said they would like Quayle replaced on the 1992 Republican ticket, although Bush has declared publicly that Quayle will stay on the ticket.

As vice president, Quayle is a better bet than any other American, at least historically, to be the next occupant of the Oval Office. Since 1952, every elected vice president, except the disgraced Spiro T. Agnew, has gone on to claim his party's nomination for president. Five of the last nine presidents served as vice president—two became president after their predecessors died in office, two were elected on their own, and one followed a presidential resignation—and Quayle scarcely bothers to conceal his own electoral ambitions for the presidency in 1996.

In reporting for these articles, *The Washington Post* studied this man who could be president, exploring his past, intensively covering his activities as vice president and examining his political future. The project examined his missions for the administration on Capitol Hill and on the Republican banquet circuit, his quasi-executive work as head of the National Space Council and the increasingly controversial White House Council on Competitiveness and his travels from Bulgaria to Brazil and to more than 20 U.S. cities. In addition to the sessions with Quayle, the reporting included four interviews with his wife and more than 200 with current and former colleagues, government officials, opponents, friends and critics.

The portrait that emerges may cause some people to feel more comfortable about the prospect of Quayle's becoming president, while leading others to dread it even more. But it is clear that—all jokes aside—Dan Quayle has proved himself to be a skillful player of the political game, with a competitive drive that has been underestimated repeatedly by his rivals.

Quayle is exposed almost daily to Oval Office discussions and decisions on vital national and international issues, and his input appears to be valued by Bush, especially on political and congressional strategy, although he is overshadowed as a force in the administration by Bush's first-tier advisers, particularly Secretary of State James A. Baker III, national security adviser Brent Scowcroft, budget director Richard G. Darman and the White House chief of staff, formerly John H. Sununu, now Samuel K. Skinner.

But to the distress of some close associates, Quayle too often skates on the surface of issues, seeming almost to revel in the traditional busywork of the No. 2 job as he flits among Republican banquets, photo opportunities and countless ceremonial appearances. "The vice president," said one who works with him closely, "walks by things instead of stopping to savor or understand them."

Quayle conceded that "when the circuits are overloaded, it takes away from the opportunity to have a serious understanding of the situation at hand." Marilyn Quayle maintained it is "frustrating for Dan" when he has as many as 12 scheduled events a day.

Quayle's close associates often question his depth and power of concentration. They also note that he is remarkably stubborn or indolent about his seeming inability to read a speech with proper inflection and self-assurance, which he acknowledges limits his effectiveness in communicating to large audiences.

But they also know that what has sustained his political rise is his outgoing, gregarious personality—most apparent in small groups, where he most often shines.

Certain strains of conservatism, including an intense distrust of bureaucracy, are clear in his thinking. But his victories as a politician reflect his adaptability and tactical acumen rather than a consistent ideological vision. He is intensely partisan, although old political rivals attest to his personal decency, and he shows little instinct for the jugular. "He's not a natural nut-cutter," according to one ally.

He enjoys sports and locker-room camaraderie as much as any man in public life and is quick, when the sun shines and a friend calls, to chuck his job for a round of golf. Yet he goes out of his way to acknowledge that his wife is a central and essential part of everything he does in government and politics. Politicians in the past, Marilyn Quayle said, never acknowledged that "your little wifey . . . helps you." But her husband does, she said, and "he's not embarrassed."

ASPIRING TO NATIONAL NOTICE

So many questions have been asked about why Bush picked Dan Quayle as his running mate that little attention has been focused on how Quayle put himself in the right spot to be picked.

In interviews, Quayle explained the thinking he said led him to reach for the vice presidency. "Politics is so uncertain and unpredictable that after you have two elections behind you and you've got 6 to 10 years in Congress . . . unless you want to stay there 40 years, you've got to figure out what you're going to do," he said. In February 1988, he decided it was "time to . . . roll the dice. . . . And if the vice presidency happens to come along, so be it."

There were earlier twinges of aspiration to national recognition. As a 37-year-old senator, he attended the 1984 Republican National Convention in Dallas and watched the floor demonstrations for Jack Kemp. On the final day, he read a Dallas newspaper story about up-and-coming young Republicans. "My name wasn't mentioned, and I was mad," Quayle recalled.

After 1986—when he was reelected to his Senate seat by what at that time was the widest margin in Indiana, even as his party was suffering serious national reverses and losing its Senate majority—Quayle explored the possibility of becoming chairman of the National Republican Senatorial Committee, a campaign post from which Barry Goldwater, among others, had moved to the presidential nomination. He backed off when his friend Sen. Don Nickles (R-Okla.)

staked a claim to the job. But he kept looking for ways to gain political altitude.

So in February 1988, after Bush won in New Hampshire, Quayle said he saw it was "time to begin to develop some wings and see if you can fly."

Over the next few months, he made more Senate floor speeches, wrote more op-ed pieces and issued more press releases than ever before, especially on high-profile issues such as defense that would become the themes of the 1988 presidential race. He spoke up in the weekly closed-door lunches of Senate Republicans, which Bush attended as vice president when he was in town, and Dole remembers seeing Quayle drop in often at Bush's office, just off the Senate floor. He spoke frequently with senior Bush campaign aides Roger Ailes and Robert M. Teeter, who had worked on Quayle's Senate campaigns. Quayle recalled even asking Ailes directly one day, "How am I doing?"

Dole, himself a vice presidential contender at that point, was not the only colleague who noticed what was going on. Sen. William S. Cohen (R-Maine) said, "It looked like there was a game plan to get Bush's attention because Quayle thought he had a shot" at the vice presidency.

Quayle also launched a low-key effort to be chosen to deliver the keynote address at the upcoming Republican convention—prime time before a national television audience. "I lobbied a little bit, very discreetly. . . . I thought I'd be . . . good," he said. But he avoided direct contact on this front with the Bush aides making the decision. Instead, he said, "I did it one step removed. I didn't want to be that direct. If I didn't get it, I didn't want to seem too pushy."

In March, even though only one news story speculating about Quayle's vice presidential chances had appeared, he had his Senate press secretary, Jeffrey A. Nesbit, say publicly that rumors that he was under consideration were "pretty substantial."

In April, Quayle proposed an alternative to a Democratic bill requiring employers to notify workers of impending plant closings, making the notification "voluntary." Bush endorsed Quayle's plan—in May the *New York Times* called it the "Quayle-Bush compromise"—and although it failed, it helped the vice president defuse what Baker, then Treasury secretary and soon to become Bush's campaign chairman, felt was a "very hot, very hot issue" for Bush to handle.

That spring, in speeches on and off the Senate floor, Quayle also raised serious warnings on the Intermediate-Range Nuclear Forces (INF) treaty the Reagan administration had negotiated with the Soviet Union. Quayle argued that the treaty language put undesirable restrictions on future technologies not yet imagined by weapons designers. This idea grew out of policy discussions held by a group of Republican senators that Quayle had formed in 1983. The group—consisting of Quayle, Pete Wilson of California, Warren B. Rudman of New Hampshire and Malcolm Wallop of Wyoming—was designed to provide a Republican counterweight to Sen. Sam Nunn's (D–Ga.) increasing domination of the defense debate. They met over lunch for two-hour sessions with a range of experts, from Carter administration national security adviser Zbigniew Brzezinski to Secretary of Defense Caspar W. Weinberger and

Admiral William J. Crowe, Jr., chairman of the Joint Chiefs of Staff.

When the INF treaty was introduced in the Senate, Quayle initially opposed it and later urged that it be modified to meet his concerns about future technologies. Sen. Alan K. Simpson (R–Wyo.), the Minority Whip, recalled cornering Quayle in the back of the Senate chamber one day and telling him: "You're driving me crazy. You're really putting the blocks to me. What is it you want?"

"And boy, he just stood right there, and his blue eyes were flashing, and he said, 'I'll tell you what I want. This, this, this and this. And till that gets in there, this son of a bitch isn't going anywhere,' " Simpson recalled.

In the end Quayle voted for the treaty, but because of the objections he and others raised, the Reagan administration had to go back to the Soviet Union to clarify the question of futuristic technologies. A binding condition on this point was ultimately added to the treaty text that put restrictions on future weapons. Though it was not what Quayle wanted, he said he was glad that the clarification would avoid treaty ambiguities.

Quayle's public efforts did not endear him to Ronald Reagan. But he solidified his relationships with the conservative network that Bush and his campaign manager, Lee Atwater, constantly were monitoring as they canvassed for vice presidential suggestions.

Even more important, in the early summer of 1988, Quayle met with Bush and urged him to press Reagan to veto the entire $300 billion defense budget bill on grounds that congressional Democrats had taken too much out of strategic weapons systems. He also argued that Congress had inserted too many policy directives on arms control and related matters that Quayle, like Bush, believed should be left to the discretion of a president.

Working behind the scenes in a way that went unreported at the time, Quayle challenged the heavyweights in the Reagan administration. National security adviser Colin L. Powell, Secretary of Defense Frank C. Carlucci and Joint Chiefs chairman Crowe all were recommending that Reagan sign the bill as the best he could get. Quayle argued that if Reagan caved in and signed the bill, it would be telling the voters in 1988 that there was no difference between Republicans and Democrats on defense. "The politics were on our side on this," Quayle recalled.

He made the case directly to Bush, once with several other senators, then with former senator John G. Tower (R-Tex.), at his side. "Even more so than Tower, I was adamant" that the bill should be vetoed, Quayle said. Bush took that message to the president, and Reagan vetoed the bill in early August, just 13 days before Bush picked Quayle for vice president. As Quayle had predicted, the veto underscored the differences between the parties and highlighted the Republicans' pro-defense position at a critical time in the presidential campaign.

Quayle said he believes "that was the turning, that was the major point" in his relationship with Bush. "I was with him [Bush] actively urging him to urge Reagan to veto the defense bill.

"I talked to him on the phone periodically but I had the kind of relationship where I could, I felt very comfortable calling, saying, 'George, I need to talk to you about this.' Or, 'Here's what I think you ought to do.' "

Quayle's position on the defense veto, a close aide at the time recalled recently, "had an intended audience of one: Bush."

Although Quayle was not chosen to give the convention keynote speech, he said Bush was aware of the six-month attention-getting effort. Quayle was invited to at least two briefing sessions with Bush at the vice president's residence. Bush "certainly noticed what we were doing and paid attention . . . all along," Quayle recalled.

President Bush declined to be interviewed about Quayle. But in the spring of 1988, said then Indiana governor Robert D. Orr and state Republican chairman Gordon Durnil, Bush visited Indiana on a campaign swing and—to their surprise—seemed very interested in learning more about Quayle.

"We had this long discussion about how Quayle was perceived," Durnil said in a recent interview. He said Bush asked, "Why does he do well with female voters? Is it just because he's cute?" Durnil said he told Bush that, no, it had more to do with Quayle's ability to make eye contact with all voters and not to pass by women voters to get to their check-writing husbands.

Orr said he told Bush that Quayle was particularly popular with young voters and that he had an approval rating higher than Sen. Richard G. Lugar, the state's senior Republican senator.

Meanwhile, Dan and Marilyn Quayle kept their own scorecard. They reviewed the names of possible Bush running mates, adding and subtracting people over the months, identifying the criteria they thought Bush was using. They liked the odds. Quayle sensed that the selection would turn as much on the disqualifiers for other contenders as the qualifiers.

"I knew what the competition was," he said, "and I always thought I was pretty good."

Quayle acknowledged that others might have thought he should stay put, gain some seasoning in the Senate, show some patience, become wiser. But Quayle knew that Richard M. Nixon and both Roosevelts had been nominated or elected vice president at roughly his age—Nixon at 39, Theodore Roosevelt at 42 and Franklin D. Roosevelt, an unsuccessful candidate at 38.

"Well, it wasn't too soon for" them, Quayle said. "A lot of politics is timing. Timing and opportunity. And the two are critical to success but you can't necessarily determine either one of them."

There was another factor—ambition. Quayle doesn't use the word, but he calls the vice presidency a "career advancement."

THE CALL COMES FROM BUSH

At 8 A.M. on July 25, 1988, the Monday after the windup of the Democratic National Convention, when polls showed Bush trailing Michael S. Dukakis by 17 points, came the first clear proof that Quayle had not misjudged the situation. George Bush picked up the phone and called Quayle's office. Quayle had not yet arrived from his home in McLean, but he returned the call within a half hour.

"I remember exactly what he said," Quayle recalled. "He asked if he could consider me [among others] to be his vice presidential nominee. Monday morning. Called my office."

Quayle played it cool, telling Bush, "I'm flattered, but I wanted to think about it for 24 hours." What he really wanted to do was talk it over with his wife.

"The one person I talked to was Marilyn . . . I didn't talk to any others for advice."

Family comes first for the Quayles, not just rhetorically in the speeches they both give, but in the ordering of their daily lives. During dinner that evening, they told their children—Tucker, Benjamin and Corinne—of the call. "They're tight-lipped," said the ever-practical Marilyn Quayle, "so that was no problem.

"We discussed what it would mean to the family if he were chosen and whether we were willing to do that," she said. "The kids were still young enough that I don't think, other than Tucker [then 14], they really comprehended one way or the other."

Quayle's first goal had been reached—he was on the list. When the children left the table, Dan and Marilyn Quayle sat down to assess his chances of becoming Bush's final choice, and the nation's 44th vice president.

"He wouldn't have called Dan if he wasn't really considering him," Marilyn Quayle said. "This wasn't just a fly-by-night call, a stroke call, one of the ones you have to do." If Bush had simply wanted another midwesterner on the list besides Dole, then Lugar, as former chairman of the Senate Foreign Relations Committee, was the plausible choice.

Marilyn Quayle—as analytical as her husband is intuitive in political judgments—laid out the reasons Bush might pick him. As she recalled recently, they were: "The generational thing. The Midwest. The fact that Dan had such a strong defense background. What he'd done with JTPA [the Job Training Partnership Act, which Quayle sponsored and got passed as a freshman senator], which helped on the social front a great deal."

Add in the fact "that they wouldn't have some of the personality conflicts that some of the other people brought into it," like Dole and Kemp, both of whom had opposed Bush for the presidential nomination. And "that all the people [Bush] had advising him professionally—Teeter, Ailes—had worked with Dan and knew what he was able to do.

"Compared to everyone else," Marilyn Quayle said they concluded that night, "it just made sense." As a "choice people wouldn't expect," it would also help Bush fight his reputation of "always doing the status quo, [being] the wimp," and the perception "that he will never get out on a limb on anything."

"We did all the pros and cons . . . and pretty much decided then . . . that Dan was probably the one he should pick. People think that's just absolutely insane, but we really did," she said. Her husband would "give the most punch to the ticket."

The next morning Quayle called the vice president to say he would be "flattered, flattered" to be considered.

GETTING THE WORD OUT

Quayle knew Bush wanted to keep his short list secret. "There was an understanding that he did not want this out," he recalled. "I wasn't going to let it leak out."

But within a few days, other names on the list were appearing in the news media, and Nesbit remembered "Dan was sort of angry that there were all these names out there and not his."

Quayle contacted Bush, and said, "Everyone else has said that they've been contacted. Is it all right for me?" With Bush's agreement, Nesbit released the information to the Indiana news media for publication on Friday, July 29.

The next day, Quayle was sitting beside the pool in McLean with his friend Kenneth L. Adelman, Reagan's former arms control director. Quayle told Adelman the news.

"We should have a little boomlet over this," Adelman said. "You know, get your name around, talk to editorial boards, get a list of 15 important people to see and talk to."

"Adelman thought I ought to have some notoriety," Quayle recalled. "And I said, 'We don't want too much notoriety. This is not going to be a selection where George Bush is going to read the press reports and decide on that [basis] who is going to be his vice presidential nominee.' "

Still, Adelman talked up Quayle and, with Nesbit's help, drafted a column for the Wednesday, August 10, *Washington Times*, headlined "Why not Sen. Dan Quayle?"

Calling Quayle a "dark horse," Adelman wrote that the senator could help Bush with "Reagan Democrats, women, and young voters and in the Midwest." He noted that Quayle "is a true conservative on abortion, school busing, prayer in the schools." The published column was read and portions were underlined by Bush.

As the GOP convention neared, Quayle sent six close aides and friends to New Orleans. According to one, William R. Neale, they printed up about 200 placards and another 200 buttons saying "Bush-Quayle," just in case.

ABC asked him to appear on "This Week with David Brinkley" the Sunday before the convention. "Everyone kept saying, 'No, don't do it. You don't campaign for it,' " Quayle recalled. Marilyn Quayle and all of his staff were opposed to the appearance. Baker, about to take over as head of Bush's campaign, also told Quayle to say no.

But columnist George Will, a regular on the show, called Quayle in Indiana to urge him to appear, informing him that Dole and Kemp would be on the program. Quayle said he "made a snap decision . . . that I was going to do it. . . . I had been so scrupulous in . . . abiding by this low-key thing that I felt one good shot at an opportune time would be appropriate."

Quayle told the national television audience that included Bush that he understood the rules for No. 2 on the ticket. Whoever Bush picked for his running mate, Quayle said, would realize that "the themes, the issues, the articulation on the campaign will be George Bush's."

Forty-eight hours later, Bush announced Quayle's selection, and America was introduced to the stranger who had positioned himself to become the president's understudy.

2. The Roots of a Route
to Washington

1976–1980

Dan Quayle in grade school (left) and in his Huntington, Indiana, 1965 high school graduation picture (right).

Marilyn and Dan Quayle after they received their law degrees from Indiana University–Indianapolis Law School in 1974. Marilyn Tucker, the enormously disciplined daughter of two physicians, was introduced to Dan Quayle in 1972 and married him after a ten-week courtship.

PRECEDING PAGE—(Left) Representative Quayle pumping gasoline in Indiana in 1980 to demonstrate his opposition to a tax proposed by President Jimmy Carter. (Right) Eugene C. Pulliam, the newspaper publisher who once warned his grandson never to trust a politician.

The story of Dan Quayle's entry into politics in 1976 at the age of 29 has been told dozens of times. In it, Orvas Beers, the Republican county chairman in Fort Wayne, Indiana, and Ernie Williams, editor of the *Fort Wayne News-Sentinel,* meet an unsuspecting Quayle—then associate publisher of the 8,300-circulation *Herald-Press* in Huntington—at a Friday luncheon and out of the blue invite him to run for Congress.

Quayle, the story goes, is thunderstruck. He has never considered political office before. "You mean now?" he asks. He demurs; he must get his father's permission. The tale invariably ends with Quayle, nine months later, being handed the House seat, like so much else in his life, on a silver platter.

In the popular version of Quayle's ascent, someone—an Orvas Beers or an Ernie Williams, his well-connected father, James C. Quayle, or his powerful grandfather, newspaper baron Eugene C. Pulliam—provides the impetus and the means for the unambitious lad to do it all. According to this view, George Bush is Quayle's ultimate political godfather, anointing the previously obscure senator as his 1988 running mate.

It is a nice, simple version of events. But it is largely fable. Among other things, it ignores his calculations, and the vital role of his wife, Marilyn Quayle, in his ascent.

True, Quayle did not know when he walked into the Fort Wayne Press Club for lunch that day that he would be offered the nomination. But he has always operated on the principle, as he put it in a recent interview, that you try to "put yourself in a position to make decisions and keep doors open."

After graduating from Indiana University Law School-Indianapolis in 1974, he turned down job offers from law firms and government offices in the state capital, choosing instead to help run the small newspaper owned by his father in the town where he had spent part of his childhood.

The selection of Huntington, Quayle said, "wasn't an accident"; it was a political calculation. Anti-Indianapolis sentiment abounded in the state at that time, and Indiana, he knew, had not elected a statewide candidate from the capital for a long time. Huntington, he felt, "would be my best political opportunity."

Even within Huntington, he chose his spot with care. When Dan and Marilyn Quayle picked out a home, he said, he intentionally chose one in a district whose state representative was a Democrat. "I actually had my eye on that [seat] more than I did the Congress."

For the first two decades of his life, Dan Quayle did not impress anyone as a good bet to win much of anything but a golf game. His performance as a student was weak, his grades at best mediocre. The competitiveness and calculation that later marked his political rise were camouflaged by the comfort provided by his family.

Quayle was born in Indianapolis in 1947 to James and Corinne Quayle. Jim Quayle was a middle manager with the newspaper chain owned by his father-in-law, Eugene Pulliam, first in Huntington (pop. 16,000), the classic midwestern small town that Dan Quayle calls his home, and then in Arizona, where the Quayles moved when Dan was eight. In 1963, when Dan was 16, Jim Quayle, a far-right conservative and member of the John Birch Society, bought the *Huntington Herald-Press* from his father-in-law, and the family moved back there for Dan's last two years of high school.

Though Gene Pulliam had made a fortune, he did not believe in inherited wealth. Dan Quayle grew up as a child of middle-class privilege, very protected but not pampered: country clubs but public schools. His family's homes were modest. During their first stay in Huntington, the Quayles lived in a small, white, one-story house; after returning in 1963, they moved into a standard two-story brick suburban-style house with a two-car garage.

"The most expensive vacation I took with my mother and father was a two-week trip from Phoenix, Arizona, up to

Idaho," Quayle said. "We camped out. It was a 1960 white [Nash] Rambler station wagon. We pulled a tent trailer with a fold-out tent that we flipped up. We cooked every meal except two." One restaurant outing came about only because "gasoline spilled on the compartment where my mother fixed sandwiches."

Nonetheless, someone as close to Quayle as his former aide and Senate successor, Dan Coats, observed that "standing back and looking at the surface of his life, almost everyone would say it was fairly sheltered, some would say privileged. Plenty of opportunities to play golf; enough money in the family to live a comfortable lifestyle. . . . Nothing really on the surface that would have seemed to develop that drive and spirit in him."

Beneath the surface, however, there were forces that made it harder for Dan Quayle just to coast. His father, a warm-hearted, convivial man whose personality is reflected in his son, was viewed by many intimates as living in a kind of probationary status among his wife's success-oriented relatives, who placed him in what one calls "the outer orbits of the Pulliam empire."

Quayle recalled that when he was 10, his father had a serious variety of the disease lupus, which can affect the vital organs. "He was in the hospital and I remember I over-heard my mother talking to someone on the phone, saying, 'Well, they can pack Jim's stuff at the office and put it in the closet.' Which meant that he was never going back to work."

His mother turned to him, the oldest of four children, for assistance. The Quayles had just adopted twins, a boy and a girl, who were a year old. Quayle said he changed their diapers and helped cook for the family during the two years his father was in and out of the hospital. "It was a real struggle. Very difficult time. For her, for all of us."

Marilyn Quayle said, "He really is the one that held the family together."

AN EARLY INTEREST IN POLITICS

More than power or money, what Quayle inherited from his family was an obsession with politics. Quayle recalled that at age 12 or 13 he trailed his grandfather and President Dwight D. Eisenhower as they played nine holes of golf. His mother served as a precinct committeewoman in Arizona, and his father's newspaper work was intertwined with politics.

The landmark Republican events of Quayle's youth are etched in his mind: Sen. Barry Goldwater's 1958 reelection campaign; the shock when Democrat Birch Bayh won a Senate seat from Indiana in 1962; the 1968 Republican National Convention in Miami that Quayle, then age 21, attended as a driver for Richard M. Nixon's minions. Although Nixon won the nomination in Miami, Quayle said, "[Ronald] Reagan was the one that captured the heart of that convention."

In high school, Quayle paid more attention to politics—
and to golf, his number-one interest—than to classes.
According to his high school guidance counselor, his grades
were not good enough to assure him a place in the class of
1969 at DePauw University, which his grandfather and
both his parents had attended. But he was admitted as a
"legacy" with direct Pulliam family connections. Though
Jim Quayle paid the bills, he wouldn't provide what Dan
considered sufficient spending money, so Dan ran the
laundry account at his Deke fraternity house.

Every Sunday night he would make the rounds of his
brothers to collect "everybody's fluff"—underwear and T-
shirts, Quayle said. He would ask about their dress shirts:
"Would you like these ironed? You want these in boxes or
do you want them on hangers? You want starch, light
starch?"

He said, "I just wanted some extra spending money.
. . . I wasn't going to not eat or anything like that. But I did
it on my own. It was a good job. . . . I've never had to be a
beggar, that's for sure."

Quayle graduated from DePauw in 1969 with a C average. It was the height of the Vietnam War, and Quayle
joined the Indiana National Guard rather than risk being
drafted because, he said, he wanted to go to law school.
According to Marilyn Quayle, he had been unfocused in
his life plans before then. "If I'd met him in college, I never
ever would have even gone out with him." But, she said, six
months of basic training awakened him, and made him say,
" 'Okay, now it is time for me to be an adult. I've got to

decide what I'm going to do with myself, and I've got to make a difference.'

"That was that six-month basic training, crawling on his belly, learning to weld," she said. "That was really his transition point."

Quayle agreed. "You go, 'Oh, hello world.' Hey, it's an eye-opener."

Admitted to the IU-Indianapolis Law School in 1970 despite his mediocre undergraduate record, he began to buckle down somewhat, combining classes with political jobs in the state attorney general's and governor's offices. For the first time, although his grades remained less than impressive, teachers and mentors such as then-state senator Robert D. Orr began describing Quayle as "quick and willing to work."

In 1972 he met Marilyn Tucker, the enormously disciplined daughter of two physicians, a Purdue University graduate who was also studying law at IU-Indianapolis.

They were introduced by Bill Neale, a fellow student who had known Marilyn Tucker since grade school. Ten weeks after they started dating, they were married.

FEARING HIS WIFE'S REACTION

It was in part his wife's reaction that Quayle had in mind when he told Beers and Williams, at lunch that 1976 day in

Fort Wayne, "I'm really not sure that I am ready to run for Congress. . . . If I was going to run for anything this year, I might be running for that state representative seat down there."

But he also did a quick political calculation. Before he would risk the tougher race against Democratic incumbent J. Edward Roush, who had served 16 years in Congress, certain conditions would have to be met.

First, Quayle asked Beers to keep all competition out of the primary. Quayle said recently that he knew Beers couldn't guarantee him a clear shot at the nomination, "but I wanted to test him." In fact, Beers did discourage all but what he calls "the fruitcakes" and "fringe candidates" from challenging Quayle. On May 4, Quayle trounced his lone primary opponent 63 to 37 percent.

Second, Quayle said, he asked Beers "to look me in the eye and guarantee me the money" for such a challenge. And that Beers was able to do.

Press accounts at the time described Quayle's run as a "dress rehearsal" for 1978. "Not true," Quayle said. "When you run, you run hard, and you expect to win." No one argued, however, with Quayle's recollection that "except for me and Marilyn and maybe one or two other people . . . [no one] thought we could win."

After talking to Beers and Williams that Friday, Quayle drove with his wife to a weekend newspaper conference in Williamsburg, Virginia. Quayle said he waited until they were in Ohio to tell her that he might run.

He clearly had reason to fear her reaction. When the law

school classmates met and married, Marilyn Quayle said in a recent interview, she believed he was "adamant" that he was "definitely not a politician" but a "lawyer-businessman" who hoped to acquire a chain of newspapers and "hit politics from that side, rather than as an elected official."

Told in a subsequent interview that his wife said "politics was the furthest thing from his mind" when she married him, Quayle laughed and said, "Well, maybe it was further from hers than from mine."

In the fall of 1991, as Quayle was telling the story of that 1976 auto trip, mimicking Marilyn Quayle's voice saying, " 'You told me you were never going to get into politics,' " the door to his formal office in the Old Executive Office Building opened and his wife walked in.

"We were debating on whether I really ever told you that I'd never go into politics," he said to her.

"Yep. You did," she said.

Dan Quayle laughed. "Not, I mean, not never."

"You said you'd never—and I have witnesses. You said you'd never run for Congress."

"See, I said that. I told them that. It was the Congress thing that I—"

"You'd never run for Congress," Marilyn Quayle repeated, as her husband vainly tried to complete the thought. "You said you might run for the state senate, but it would be a long way off . . . after we'd established [our] business and [had] kids and things, but never run for Congress."

Dan Quayle leaned forward, waving his hands, as if asking for time out. But his wife pressed on. "You said you'd prefer to be influential like your grandfather—behind the scenes."

In a solo interview, Quayle said, "She knew I was interested in politics. She was interested in politics! . . . Bottom line, she supported it. . . . She was my best campaign adviser, and very involved."

CAMPAIGNING THEIR OWN WAY

The race was tough. It was two years after Watergate and President Gerald R. Ford was on his way to defeat, though he carried Indiana and Quayle's Fourth District. The once-powerful Fort Wayne GOP organization had splintered into factions, and Quayle's first task was to assemble a "Quayle Quartet" of senior advisers, representing all the warring groups.

He and Marilyn decided to open a Quayle-for-Congress office separate from the Republican headquarters. The party veterans bristled. "We did not think it was wise," Beers recalled. Worse, the Quayles decided not to mention the word "Republican" anywhere in his campaign literature. "He ought to let them know he's a Republican," said Beers. Quayle said he shot back, "Do you want to win this election or not?"

Jimmy Carter's success in the spring and summer of 1976 had caught Quayle's eye and he decided to appropriate elements of the Democratic nominee's "outsider" message. He even printed his posters, signs and literature in Carter green.

"I ran a somewhat populist campaign," Quayle said. "Washington's wrong. Anti-busing, anti-welfare, anti–big government. I was saying a lot of the things Carter was saying, but I was saying it as a Republican."

The National Republican Congressional Committee took a look at Quayle's race and was not impressed enough to send any early money. But the nominee spent a weekend in Milwaukee, where Paul Weyrich, head of the New Right's Free Congress Foundation, was conducting a campaign school with Bob Kasten, now senator from Wisconsin.

They preached the "Kasten Plan" of intensive precinct organization, derived from AFL-CIO campaign manuals, and emphasized the political value of tapping new constituencies opposed to abortion, the Equal Rights Amendment and gun control.

Marilyn Quayle took control of organizing the race, though she was well along in her second pregnancy. "I liked it," she recalled. "It's like preparing for a trial. . . . It's that kind of strategic planning I like."

She appointed herself the liaison to the Republican organization leaders, and they met Friday afternoons in the back room of Mother's Restaurant in Fort Wayne. "I was always there," she said. "Dan was out campaigning. I was the one that met with the county chairmen and stroked everybody and made everybody fall into place . . . and did all of the organizational things."

Her role—and the assertiveness with which she played it—did not sit well with the Old Guard Republicans. Many of them felt she complained too much.

Paul Helmke, a GOP campaign worker and now the mayor of Fort Wayne, recalled: "She had lots of comments. There was a nervousness about her; she was concerned about money. She was concerned about the crazy schedule. . . . She would say things like, 'I'm not hearing the advertising enough. I'm not hearing the jingle.' "

Alan McMahan, the city GOP chairman in Fort Wayne for the past 25 years, said, "The idea that a wife could have this influence and intelligence, have ideas of her own, was foreign to the power establishment here." Marilyn Quayle agreed. "They were astonished from the beginning that Dan . . . felt very comfortable that I could represent him completely. That was shocking to them," she said.

With some, it still rankles. If Marilyn Quayle said she used those Fridays at Mother's for "stroking" sessions, said Richard Fishering, Beers's deputy in the county organization, "I think she is full of shit, as usual."

The disrespect is mutual. In an interview, Marilyn Quayle dismissed the Old Guard as "a bunch of little boys who were used to doing things their own way," and blamed them for "the real erosion of the Republican Party in the Fourth District," which is now represented in the House by Democrat Jill Long.

McMahan called Marilyn Quayle "the driving force" in the campaign and said, "She brought a consistency to what he [Dan] was going to say. She had a firm hand, and it was necessary" to keep the campaign on track.

Walter Helmke, an Indiana state senator who had run unsuccessfully for the congressional seat in 1974, also emphasized her role in choosing the issues. He said that early in the year, "Quayle had no formulated opinion" on social issues. "What Marilyn did was formulate the issues for Dan. She came in and told us he is going to adopt a pro-life stance. He is adopting the position of the NRA [National Rifle Association]. And he is against the Equal Rights Amendment. . . . I've always felt that she felt more strongly about these issues than he did."

Marilyn Quayle said that she and her husband had discussed these issues "at home at night" before she shared her views with others, and insisted that "he felt a lot more strongly about some of those things than I did." But she does not seek to diminish her own role.

"I ran the meetings, made them listen, shot down their ideas when they came up and," she added, "made them feel a part of the whole process, which is what I was supposed to do. . . . It never occurred to me that those men would sit there and not treat me as an equal or as someone who was going to tell them what to do. That was my role."

No one had to tell Quayle how to run against Big Government and Washington. From his grandfather and his father, he had learned that bureaucracy and regulation, taxes and spending were prime evils. Fifteen years before it became a national issue, Quayle argued for congressional term limits. He assailed Roush for supporting such things as the bailout of New York City.

The incumbent was puzzled—and unprepared. "He called it a giveaway," Roush remembered of Quayle's incessant attack on the New York loan guarantee. "You couldn't tell him it would be paid back."

Yet Roush, like Quayle's later opponents, stipulated that Quayle never made personal attacks. "I found him to be a fair campaigner," Roush said. "There was nothing below the belt."

In the end, Quayle, aided by contributions from New Right political action committees, outspent Roush two to one and vastly out-campaigned him. On small-town Main Streets, at Friday night football games, in the laundromats and bowling alleys, Quayle shook hands and flashed his smile through 16-hour days, and recruited the precinct-walking volunteers whose names filled Marilyn Quayle's shoe boxes.

Pollster Robert M. Teeter, now chairman of the 1992 Bush-Quayle reelection campaign, had seen one Republican after another—most with better paper credentials than Quayle—fail to dislodge Roush. "They [the Quayles] did it," he said. "I mean they went out and did thoroughly all the work anybody ever suggested and more. I mean, they persevered!"

On election night, Quayle beat Roush by 19,000 votes, a 55 to 45 percent edge. At 29, Dan Quayle was going to Congress. But that was only the first step he and his wife had in mind.

SETTING SIGHTS ON THE SENATE

In the middle of 1977, just six months after he started in the House, the Quayles began planning the shift to the Senate.

Birch Bayh, the third-term Democratic incumbent with a liberal voting record, was a thorn in the flesh of Hoosier Republicans, especially conservatives such as Gene Pulliam. Since Bayh ousted Sen. Homer Capehart (R) as a youth of 34 in 1962, he had narrowly defeated two of the best-credentialed GOP challengers, Richard G. Lugar, now the state's senior senator, and William Ruckelshaus, who later became deputy attorney general and head of the Environmental Protection Agency (EPA).

Long before Pulliam could have guessed that his grandson would accomplish that feat, he had given young Dan Quayle an important political lesson—using Bayh as his subject.

The instruction came on Memorial Day weekend in 1970 at the Highland Golf Course, when Quayle was playing a round with his grandfather. A day earlier, the crowd at the Indianapolis 500 auto race had booed Bayh as he was introduced. Quayle, then 23, asked if his grandfather had heard of the incident.

Laughing, Pulliam said he had just written an editorial bawling out the people of Indiana for showing no respect for their senator, and expressing shock and dismay at the "display of atrociously bad manners."

What? Quayle asked, disbelieving. Bayh was the symbol of everything the Pulliams opposed. "We got into a big altercation on the first tee," Quayle recalled recently.

You don't understand, Pulliam explained. "If I would have gone out there and attacked Birch Bayh and said that the crowd deserved to boo him, I wouldn't look good." Chiding the crowd raised Pulliam's credibility while reminding everyone of the embarrassment to Bayh. "I took the absolute reverse," Pulliam added, "but the message got through."

As Quayle recalled, "All of a sudden I stood there and realized, you know, he's exactly right."

Politics, he came to see, is often a game of indirection, achieving results through carefully calibrated, self-protective, small moves aimed at a larger goal, without letting superficial contradictions get in the way of practical needs. "My grandfather told me never to trust a politician," Quayle remarked, "although they were some of his best friends."

Quayle began planning his challenge to Bayh soon after he had defeated Roush in 1976. James Loomis, a business executive and the finance chairman of that first House campaign, recalled sitting with the new congressman shortly after his election and hearing him say that if he could win reelection to his congressional seat in 1978 with more than 60 percent of the vote, and no other leading Indiana Republican wanted to run against Bayh, he could have a shot. Confirming the story, Quayle said, "I knew I had to have over 60 percent."

Running in 1978 against Democratic attorney John Walda, Quayle got 66 percent. He also began to move statewide. "I campaigned in a couple other congressional districts, which is very unusual in Indiana. . . . I thought I was in pretty good shape to take time out of my campaign . . . knowing full well that 1980 was not too far around the corner. And I wanted again to put myself in a position to be able to make that decision."

Quayle's efforts did not go unnoticed. On election night in 1978, Quayle said, he was approached by Beers and another Fourth District GOP veteran. They told him not to get too inflated a notion of himself and that, when it came to the Senate, "there are a lot of people in line before you, and you just stay where you are."

He had no trouble ignoring their advice. He didn't like being a junior member of the Republican minority in the House. He was part of a post-Watergate generation impatient with Democratic domination of the committee and floor agendas, and with older Republicans' orthodoxy. Like his friends Trent Lott and Jack Kemp, Quayle was stirred by Ronald Reagan's efforts to redefine conservatism and was eager to play on a larger field. "I always considered him a comrade in arms," Kemp recalled, "but not at the epicenter of the growth wing of the party." Quayle's principal committee assignment was Foreign Affairs, far removed from the economic battleground, and while he enjoyed the subject matter, he had little seniority or influence on its work.

"He wasn't able to get anything done," said Marilyn Quayle. "He felt like he was beating his head against the wall." Or, as colleagues from House days would put it, sweating out his frustration with long hours in the House gym.

A few weeks after the 1978 victory, Quayle, his father and four friends and advisers gathered in the Indianapolis apartment of David Griffiths, a law school classmate of Dan and Marilyn. Three of the six had worked for Gov. Otis "Doc" Bowen, the Republican incumbent, and they discussed the possibility that Bowen would want the opportunity to challenge Bayh in 1980.

Quayle recalled: "I said, 'What incentive is there for Doc Bowen, [who has] been in elective politics since the early 1950s, former speaker of the [Indiana] House, two-term popular governor from the state of Indiana, that he would want to go out and be the junior senator from Indiana' " in his 60s?

In addition, Bowen's wife was terminally ill with cancer, and several suspected he might not want a campaign that would take him away from her.

But if Bowen did decide to run, Quayle knew he would have to defer to the elder Republican. So he devised a strategy of visiting key Indiana Republicans, asking for their support as a backup to Bowen.

"In '79, he came to see me," said Orr, who became Bowen's successor as governor, "and to my surprise said he was interested in running for the Senate. He told me he had gone to see Doc Bowen and told him that if Doc wanted to run, he would be his most enthusiastic supporter, but if not, he wanted to run against Birch himself.

For a fellow who was supposed not to be smart, it was an awfully smart way to approach it."

In similar conversations with what he said were 50 or 60 of Indiana's 92 county chairmen, Quayle essentially locked up the second-choice votes of most of the state's key Republicans. He even had it emblazoned on campaign buttons: "If not Bowen, then Quayle."

On May 8, 1979, Bowen announced that he would not be running, and, as Quayle recalled, "Doc mentioned my name first out of about 30 others that were potential Senate candidates." Only six days later, with dozens of pledges of support and with money in the bank left over from his House campaigns, Quayle declared his candidacy.

The 1980 contest turned out to be a repeat of 1976, with Quayle charging that Bayh was out of step with Indiana after 18 years in Washington. "They were very similar themes that I used in 1980 and that I used in 1976," Quayle said.

The result, too, was the same: a shocking upset by the little-known Quayle of an entrenched incumbent. With Ronald Reagan atop the national ticket, Quayle defeated Bayh 54 to 46 percent.

"Life has been very good to me," Quayle told a *Washington Post* reporter who profiled him just after his arrival in the Senate in early 1981. "I never had to worry about where I was going to go. But I do say, 'Dan, you know, sometime in life there's going to be a tragedy.' " It would be seven more years before George Bush gave Quayle a chance to taste adversity.

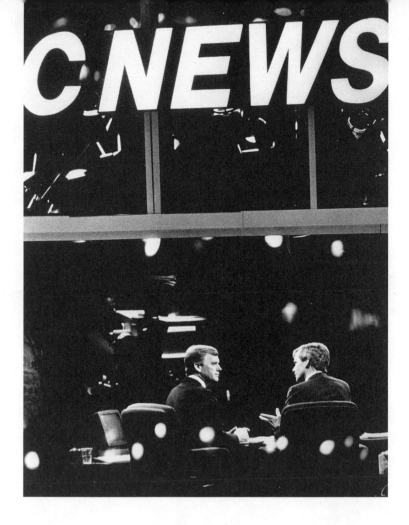

3. *"Control Freak Loses Control"*

1988

(Above) The family cheers Quayle's acceptance speech in 1988.
(Below) The family in a recent photograph: Benjamin, 15,
Corinne, 12, and Tucker, 17, with their parents.

PRECEDING PAGE—Quayle
was sent to tour four television anchor booths the day
after he was named as
Bush's choice for vice president, but in interviews,
including one with Tom
Brokaw of NBC, he raised
more questions than he
answered.

F or 12 years in politics before 1988, Dan Quayle had set his own timetables, run his own campaigns and picked his own issues. Having prospered politically by calling his own plays, with guidance only from his wife, Marilyn Quayle, he says without embarrassment, "I am a total control person."

But on Tuesday, August 16, 1988, when presidential candidate George Bush announced at the Republican National Convention in New Orleans that the 41-year-old Indiana senator was his surprise choice for running mate, Quayle lost control of his fate. Catapulted onto a careening political toboggan ride, he was unable to break his plunge, and was left at election time less than three months later a shaken man with a tattered reputation.

"He really didn't understand what he was getting into," said Stuart Spencer, the veteran California campaign consultant who managed the vice presidential effort. "He didn't understand the enormity of it."

Quayle does not quarrel with that judgment. In an interview, he agreed that the headline for the story of his 1988 campaign could be "Control Freak Loses Control."

"I just miscalculated," Quayle said. "And perhaps overestimated my skills, underestimated some of their [Spencer's and the other assigned handlers'] tendencies. And did not have a good understanding of what the national political scene was going to demand of me. I didn't handle things as well as I should have."

Quayle had worked for six months to be picked by Bush. He knew he was on the short list and was convinced he was the logical choice. Yet at the critical moment, he was not ready. After Bush called his hotel room at the convention to tell him he had been chosen, Quayle said, he jumped in the shower, put on fresh clothes and thought, "Well, now, what am I going to say?" Quayle said he "had no notes. Because I just never really spoke from a lot of notes."

Bush's campaign, left in the dark until the last minute and surprised by his choice, was equally unprepared. The next call to Quayle that Tuesday afternoon came from campaign chairman James A. Baker III, who told the Quayles to make their way from their hotel to the Spanish Plaza, the riverside dock where Bush planned to present his running mate. Marilyn Quayle recalled her husband telling Baker: " 'I'm looking at the Spanish Plaza on TV and there are thousands of people there. There's no way you can get us there.' " But "you know how Jimmy [Baker] is," she continued. " 'Trust me. Trust me. . . . We'll find you in the crowd. We'll get you in there.'

"They didn't send a soul," she said. "Nothing." It was the first of many complaints the Quayles would have about Baker during the campaign.

Baker's recollection is that outriders were dispatched but couldn't locate the Quayles. After fighting their way through the mob, the Quayles finally reached the stage for Bush's introduction.

"You can see that I was quite excited. And probably a bit hot," recalled Dan Quayle, who has watched taped replays of that moment. "I can't remember with any degree of recollection what I said. I'm sure it was brilliant and to the point," he joked.

In fact, what he did in his first moment in the national political sun was to tell the story of a man in the crowd who said to tell Bush to "Go get 'em!" Quayle grasped Bush by the arm and shoulders again and again, and cried out to the crowd: "Let's go get 'em. All right? You got it?" Calming down a little, he said he was "honored" and "humbled," and pledged to fight for what he called "George Bush's America."

News media coverage of the event compared Quayle to a cheerleader or a game show contestant who had just won the Oldsmobile.

Quayle did not need a terribly weighty message for the nation, but he had practically no message at all. There had been no private moments to talk with Bush before the announcement. In fact, he had never had a substantive conversation with Bush about serving as his running mate, or about Quayle's role in a future administration. "We walked right up on stage," Quayle said. "Boom, that's it. And the private moment was in the car on the way back to the hotel."

Was that the chance to discuss campaign themes or strategy?

"Basically, it was a welcome aboard," Quayle said. "Big welcome to part of the family. It was much more social talk rather than a 'Gee, what do we do next?' " Back in their hotel room for several hours, Quayle called his parents, and Marilyn Quayle arranged to have their three children flown to New Orleans. "We watched a little bit of [the announcement replay] on television, chitchatted," he recalled. He assumed that somebody else was explaining him and his background to reporters.

"Every once in a while, I still flash back to that moment," Quayle said. "I know what the tie was. And the suit. The suit never fit in the first place. Didn't fit then, doesn't fit—history, as they say." But the totality of the 1988 campaign is something he prefers not to recall. He said he was "shaken" by what happened, but, with characteristic rosiness, preferred to see it as "a great learning experience." Yet he said he does not like to discuss or read about that difficult time, because it resurrects unhappy memories.

Even during the campaign, Quayle tried to shut out the unpleasantness. When the nightly television news programs aired their Quayle gaffe reports, he recalled, "I just turned the television off. I said, 'Hell, I'm not going to watch them do a job [on me],' so I'd just flick that thing off and try to ignore it."

Yet Quayle's performance in the 72 hours after his introduction as Bush's running mate etched into the minds of millions of Americans a picture of a stumbling, inarticulate young politician, struggling with questions about his military service, family background, personal wealth and academic record.

After those first three days, American voters did not get another long, serious look at Quayle until the evening of October 5, when, according to virtually all pundits and polls, he was bested by Sen. Lloyd Bentsen of Texas, the Democratic vice presidential nominee, in a 90-minute televised debate from Omaha. And after that—by deliberate design of the Bush campaign—Quayle rarely was seen again. At a meeting between campaign chairman Baker and Spencer, a senior campaign official recalled, the decision was made to "go out and bury him," by scheduling Quayle only for events likely to generate minimal national news coverage.

The snapshots that remain from the campaign—Quayle's dockside overexuberance, Quayle staring into the camera like a trapped fawn as he was bombarded with news-conference and anchor-booth questions the day after his introduction, Quayle enduring the "You're no Jack Kennedy" rebuke from Bentsen—explain much of the continuing perception of him as a lightweight and, for many, a joke.

BUSH'S SHROUD OF SECRECY

At the root of many of the problems of the 1988 campaign, insiders say, was George Bush's obsessional secrecy about his choice for a vice president. Bush declined to be interviewed for these articles.

Early that year, shortly after he had routed his rivals for the presidential nomination, Bush sent a trusted aide to check in microfilm newspaper files at Washington's main public library how previous nominees, beginning with Harry S. Truman, had announced their vice presidential selections.

Most of the names, the aide reported, had leaked to the news media before official announcements were made. Rapping the desk for emphasis, Bush declared, "I am not going to let mine leak."

He let none of his top political aides read the background checks he ordered on Quayle and the other finalists. He shielded his final choice of Quayle from everyone until he flew into New Orleans on the second day of the convention. And he decided that afternoon to announce his decision on the dock, rather than to wait 24 hours as he had originally planned.

Bush had publicly promised "suspense," and that is what he delivered. Said one of his advisers: "Bush treated it like a CIA covert mission. He would not disclose who the vice presidential selectee would be until [they] were airborne, like the case officer in the movie will not disclose the destination or mission until the plane is airborne. . . . Excessive compartmentalization yields the Bay of Pigs."

Quayle said he had known in advance that there would be shock and consternation if he were chosen. On the final weekend before the convention, while visiting at his brother-in-law's home in Paoli, Indiana, he decided to share his worries with Baker in a telephone call.

"Jim," he remembered saying, "you know if it's me, there's a lot of education that needs to be done. There's who I am, and all that." Sen. Robert J. Dole (Kan.) and then-representative Jack Kemp (N.Y.)—also on Bush's short list—had just come off campaigns for the presidential nomination and were well-known national figures. "I'm not."

According to Quayle, Baker replied, "Don't worry about it; we have that all taken care of."

Baker has recalled that Quayle phoned and asked advice on whether he should accept an invitation to appear that Sunday on ABC's "This Week with David Brinkley." Baker said no; Quayle did it anyway. Quayle mentioned that the family wealth might be a public relations problem if he were chosen, and Baker recalled saying he thought that could be handled without difficulty. But he did not remember any discussion about briefing the press on Quayle's qualifications.

Whatever the case, the campaign team had no game plan for Quayle's unveiling.

Quayle's own staff was in no position to help. When the call from Bush came, according to Mary Moses Cochran, the manager of Quayle's 1986 Senate campaign, a "frazzled" Marilyn Quayle pulled Tom Duesterberg, Quayle's administrative assistant, out of the staff room at the hotel. Duesterberg returned, Cochran said, just long enough to tell her, Quayle's press secretary Jeff Nesbit and Greg Zoeller, the director of Quayle's Indiana offices, "to lock the door, tie up the phones, and watch TV." "So here we are," Zoeller recalled, "his campaign manager, his state director and his press secretary, locked in this room in the hotel watching it on TV."

SURPRISE AND CONFUSION

James Cicconi, a Baker aide who had been designated to help the vice presidential nominee, recalled that he and Spencer were "astonished" by the choice of Quayle, and had to get someone to look up the *Congressional Quarterly* profile of the senator to find out more about him.

Many of Quayle's Senate colleagues, too, were surprised and nonplussed. A month before the convention, Bush had Sen. Mitch McConnell (R-Ky.) canvass Senate Republicans for vice presidential recommendations. Only one senator listed Quayle among his top choices, McConnell recalled.

Pete Wilson of California, probably Quayle's closest ally on the Armed Services Committee, said he ranked Quayle no higher than fourth on his list. Sen. Steve Symms of Idaho, a fellow conservative and friend, recalled telling Quayle shortly before the convention, "They aren't going to pick you, so just relax. . . . Enjoy all the good press you're getting."

Delegates and reporters at the convention were as surprised as Symms to find that Bush had picked a senator few of them even knew. They could not guess why Bush had selected Quayle—and neither Quayle's aides nor Bush staff members were prepared to tell them. The first round of news stories on the announcement conveyed the shock and confusion many delegates were expressing rather than the things about Quayle that might have led Bush to choose him.

For most of his 12 years in Congress, Quayle's press operation had been aimed at his Indiana constituents. With young children, the Quayles had shunned the Washington social scene, and he had cultivated few pals in the press corps.

Before heading to New Orleans, Nesbit had stuffed one bulging file folder of Quayle's Senate accomplishments into his suitcase. But he was being held incommunicado in the Quayle staff room. Others in the group of Indiana friends and aides who came to the convention to help Quayle had prepared a few hundred copies of an updated version of his 1986 campaign brochure to hand out at the state delegations he planned to visit. "It was not much," Zoeller recalled. "We were woefully unprepared."

But Marilyn Quayle lays the blame entirely on the Bush operatives. "They should have been ready to go with papers on exactly who Dan was," she said recently. "All of his accomplishments in the Senate . . . what he was going to bring to the ticket. . . . They should have lined up his colleagues in the Senate, and members of the House, the various governors who knew Dan. . . . Nobody was lined up. There was nothing tangible to hand to a member of the press. So people were scrounging when they shouldn't have been."

At dinner the night of August 16, Quayle discovered that he would not be in control of any aspect of his own campaign. He was introduced to Spencer and Joe Canzeri, a veteran Washington public relations man, both already picked by Baker for the vice presidential team. The conversation, Quayle recalled, was "basically Spencer and Canzeri explaining a national campaign as they saw it."

Yet Quayle did not complain about being placed with handlers he did not know, and who did not know him, because, he said, "Why rock the boat?" when he had just been asked aboard.

"I never directly raised the subject with the president [Bush] on [not having] my people. . . . I wasn't going to bother him with problems that I was going to have. That would be the last thing I wanted to do. And I made the judgment early on that I would be able to control these people. . . . Up to that point, I had always been of the opinion that I could overwhelm people—I'm not sure I've got the right word—but make them my people in a very short period of time. . . . I miscalculated. And I learned a very valuable lesson. . . . There is no substitute for having your own people."

In retrospect, Quayle said, "I think the [Bush] campaign staff gambled and felt that it was probably going to be Dole. If they had known it was going to be me, they wouldn't have picked Canzeri and Spencer," because it was a "misfit."

At a news conference with Bush on Wednesday, August 17, the morning after Quayle's selection had been announced, Quayle was battered with questions about his academic record, and whether family connections had kept him out of Vietnam by helping him secure a place in the National Guard. Quayle "looked like he'd taken a bad punch," recalled the campaign's television consultant, Roger Ailes, who had worked on Quayle's 1986 Senate race and had promoted him for the vice presidency. "That's the first time I saw that deer-in-the-headlights look. I had never seen it in 1986, and I thought, 'Oh, shit, we'd better get a hold of this thing.' "

That night, in a misguided damage-control operation, Quayle was sent out to tour the four television anchor booths at the convention. In those interviews, he said that "phone calls were made" to ease his way into the National Guard, and his recollections appeared vague enough to suggest there might be significant details he was concealing. By the time he was finished, he had raised more questions than he had answered.

In the early hours of Thursday morning, August 18, Quayle was rousted from bed and sent to be grilled on his past by the campaign's high command. Richard G. Darman, a Baker protégé who is now director of the White

House Office of Management and Budget, led the inquisition. He later said that Quayle never concealed anything from the campaign, never lied and never changed his story, except to add details as they pressed him to search his memory.

"Getting Dan . . . up at three in the morning to discuss things," said Marilyn Quayle, was "just stupid, stupid! I think there was a frenzy in the press and that kind of produced a frenzy among people who would normally be a little bit more level-thinking."

The media pack's next crack at Quayle, on Friday afternoon at a news conference in Quayle's hometown of Huntington, Indiana, became one of the ugliest confrontations in the annals of press and politics, with repeated and ever-sharper questions on the National Guard. Mitch Daniels, a Hoosier lawyer-politician who had worked on Quayle's first Senate campaign and gone on to be Ronald Reagan's White House political liaison, called the staging of the event amid a hometown crowd openly antagonistic to the reporters "a terrible mistake. It poisoned the atmosphere for another several weeks."

"There was almost a feeling of hate out there," Quayle recalled.

Quayle clearly was not ready to take on the media. Pete Wilson remembered having a glass of wine with Quayle while he was in California campaigning that fall and asking Quayle how the campaign was going. "He said, 'Pete, I've never had bad press before.' And I remember laughing because I couldn't conceive of not getting bad press and being a candidate for statewide office. And I concluded that Indiana is a different place from California."

After the Huntington debacle, Quayle returned to Washington for several days of briefings. But by then, most of the damage had been done. Back on the road, he fought constantly with handlers who wanted him to give up the off-the-cuff speaking that had worked well for him in Indiana and stick to the texts they had written.

But when Quayle was allowed to ad lib, he frequently embarrassed Bush with some of his now-famous gaffes. Commenting in a Chicago speech on the need for a strong national defense, he noted that "[Indiana University basketball coach] Bobby Knight told me this. He says, 'There is nothing that a good defense cannot beat a better offense.' . . . In other words, a good offense wins."

A few days later, Quayle called the Nazi Holocaust "an obscene period in our nation's history." Trying to explain what he meant, he added, "I didn't live in this century."

The Chicago speech incident exemplified the out-of-control character of the Quayle campaign at that point. As recounted by campaign insiders, Quayle got a draft of his defense speech from his friend Kenneth Adelman and spent a day on Capitol Hill reworking it, while some of his newly assigned handlers and defense specialists on his Senate staff quarreled among themselves over phrasing. The resulting hybrid was cleared by the Bush campaign and handed out to reporters the next morning as Quayle flew to Chicago.

But the candidate was still dissatisfied. "He didn't have much problem with the content, but he said he thought it didn't have much pizzazz, and he knew this stuff, and he really wanted to show the audience that he knew it," one of the handlers recently recalled. When the handlers discovered Quayle reworking the speech in his compartment on the plane, they argued with him, but Quayle insisted that he was going to do it his way—ad libbing when he had problems with the text.

When Stuart Spencer, policy adviser James Cicconi and several others reached the site of the speech, one aide said, "We're at the staff table in the back and we know he's going to wing it, and Cicconi tells Stu that everything we've tried to do in repairing the image is at risk. And Stu says to him, 'Well, he's got to step on his —— before he learns.'

"Afterward," this aide said, "we get back on the plane and he [Quayle] says, 'I really screwed up, didn't I?' And from that point on, he got back on the script for quite a while."

Ken Khachigian, the speechwriter recruited for Quayle by Baker and Spencer, said that "the core problem was going from one level of political discourse, where [Quayle] could be folksy and relaxed and conversational, to the ultimate level of political discourse, which is the presidential campaign."

But Darman faulted the handlers more than Quayle's inability to change his customary way of operating. "He is a youthful, take-off-your-jacket, mix-with-the-crowd [campaigner]. . . . His energy level was a plus. His unmanaged style was a plus. They [the handlers] didn't see it that way." Their approach, Darman said, was "Put him in a blue suit. Don't let him take off his jacket in a crowd. . . . Keep him behind the podium. Make him look dignified. They tried to make him into something he wasn't."

What lingers for Dan and Marilyn Quayle in their pained recollections of that fall are the humiliations, large and small, that they said were heaped upon them by the handlers.

"The campaign plane . . . was not a happy place to be," Marilyn Quayle recalled. "There really was no trust in that thing. . . . I was so happy to leave that plane and go off on my own."

When she did, she said, her problems worsened. Canzeri, she said, told her staff "we couldn't have food on the [charter] flights because it cost too much." As a result, she said, she lost nearly 14 pounds in a week and "was so thin my skirt would move around and my kick pleat would end up in the front, because there was nothing to hold it. . . . It was just awful."

Canzeri recently denied this. "This is the first time I've ever been accused of cutting a budget," he added. "I wish I'd lost 14 pounds on the campaign. I didn't because I was eating hot dogs and pizza at 1 A.M., trying to straighten things out."

AFTER DEBATE, GROWING RESENTMENT

The conflict came to a head with the televised October vice presidential debate, when Quayle's youth was a stark contrast to Bentsen's gray-haired maturity. And although Quayle made no significant misstatements during the 90-minute broadcast, he walked straight into Bentsen's haymaker by comparing his own tenure in Congress with John F. Kennedy's—something he had been coached to avoid, Quayle acknowledged in a recent interview. "Once that happened," Roger Ailes said, "I said good night."

The Quayles' resentment grew after the debate, when Baker and other campaign officials were interviewed by reporters about his performance. "Baker . . . wasn't out there calling it a victory," one of the aides who was with them that night recalled. "There are hard feelings that grew out of it, because they'd thought there were too many comments from the Washington headquarters that Quayle was a drag on the ticket."

Quayle remembered feeling that "some of our people were very, shall we say, lukewarm toward my performance" in their post-debate comments. Khachigian said that Quayle, hearing the post-debate spin, "felt that he was being let down by the whole Bush operation."

"Because the handlers all came in," Quayle recalled, and they said, " 'Oh, good, good, good! Really good! You got your points across.' And then what they said behind my back was something that obviously I found out about."

Marilyn Quayle said, "People in our party—Jim Baker, who's a very good friend—they're not good spin doctors. . . . It was really handled poorly. . . . And I told them that, as I'm sure you've been told."

But she blamed the news media as much as the handlers for their problems throughout the campaign. They "were truly animals," she said of reporters. "It was shocking. I had not seen human beings behave that way around others. . . . Nobody could stand back and bring reality to the situation because it just went too fast, too far. Kind of like germs rolling [out from] under a lid."

Others have agreed that the media dwelled unfairly on Quayle's missteps. Larry Sabato, a University of Virginia political scientist, found that in the first 10 days after Quayle was named, the three major television networks devoted from two-thirds to more than four-fifths of their political coverage to him. "Balance in coverage," Sabato wrote in *Feeding Frenzy,* his book on the excesses of political journalism, "was almost absent."

Richard F. Fenno Jr., a University of Rochester political scientist and author who has written extensively about Quayle's Senate career, observed that "if one wanted to prescribe a sitting-duck target for the community of political reporters who were rushing to judgment, one could hardly have improved upon J. Danforth Quayle. I believe there was a cultural—almost a tribal—element in their early reception and treatment of him."

More than anyone or anything else, however, the Quayles time and again identified Jim Baker with the incidents that caused them trouble.

It was Baker, Quayle recalled, who promised that the inevitable press inquiries about his selection would be handled.

It was Baker, Marilyn Quayle remembered, who said "Trust me" about the logistics of the waterside announcement.

It was Baker, Quayle said, who told him he would have handlers assigned to him. "He said, 'Don't worry. Whoever [Bush's choice] is, we have the best team in place already.' "

At the rehearsal session for the fateful Wednesday morning news conference in New Orleans with Bush, "Baker sort of went through all the questions; it was sort of like a checklist," Quayle said. But the matter of how Quayle arranged to join the National Guard, which was soon to dominate coverage, never came up. "Nobody asked him the obvious question," Mitch Daniels also recalled. "I mean the air was pregnant with the question 'Well, did anybody pull a string?' There were 20 big shots [from the campaign] who had a chance to ask that. And not one did. And then they all jumped on him later."

Who told him to tour the anchor booths that night? "I don't know," Quayle said, "Baker, I presume. I mean he signed off on everything." After that disaster, it was Baker who awakened Quayle in the early morning hours Thursday with instructions to dress and start answering questions from the campaign team.

Asked who told him to answer reporters' questions in Huntington that first Friday of the campaign, Quayle said, "I think it was Baker. I think it was Baker. I presume it was Baker. . . . Baker was with us, so I presume it was Baker."

Baker has said that he was involved in all these decisions, but cannot recall whether he gave specific instructions.

When he saw Baker's commentary after the October debate, Quayle said he decided he had had enough, and was going to be "my own handler." He said he spoke to Bush within the next few days, saying, "Look, you know, I just want you to know, I'll never do anything that I think will hurt you, but I really am going to do things a little bit differently, and I'm going to be speaking out."

"And I told him, 'I'm sick of it,'" Quayle recalled. "And he says, 'Fine, I know what you're feeling.' He says, 'You know what's best.'"

After the news media reported that Quayle was going to take charge, he got a call from Baker. The message, as Quayle remembers it, was blunt: "'Well, we just read . . . how you're really going to be on your own. Well, now, just, just be careful. You want to listen, you want to listen to us.'

"And I said, 'Look! Forget it! I'm talking to whoever I want to talk to. And I'm basically going to say whatever comes to mind.'"

After Quayle's declaration of independence, Spencer left the plane and was replaced by Mitch Daniels, Quayle's friend from Indiana. Senate pals and Hoosier cronies took turns traveling with Quayle, giving him companionship and moral support. With their encouragement, he dropped the barriers to the traveling press and began frequent news conferences.

But Khachigian, Cicconi and others picked by Baker remained in their jobs. And in the end, it really didn't matter much. The gaffes stopped, but from the Omaha debate until Election Day, the spotlight of media attention never again fell on Quayle.

Quayle said he took some comfort in the cynical interpretation of Bush's campaign manager. "As Lee Atwater said, 'You were the best rabbit we had. . . . Let [the press] chase you, and [they'll] stay off the important things.'"

After the election, Quayle said, he expected the news media to let up—for there to be "light at the end of the tunnel," that "I was home free."

"I was shaken a little bit during and probably right after the campaign, as anybody would be. . . . I really just felt it was going to be over. And it was my wishful thinking.

"I never anticipated that the sort of cynicism and doubt and questioning of me would continue."

To Mom and Dad:
Thanks for all
your love and
support. It was
a great year.
Love
Danny
1-4-77

4. Quayle's Reputation vs. the Record: Damaging Campaign Coverage Was Sometimes Inaccurate

The day after his introduction at the Republican Convention, Quayle spoke to the California delegation; at a news conference that same day, he was battered with questions about his academic record and service in the National Guard.

Guardsman Dan Quayle (left) in 1971. Records show there were vacancies when he joined the unit.

PRECEDING PAGE—Dan Quayle inscribed this photograph to his parents to commemorate their celebration of his first day in Washington as a congressman from Indiana.

D an Quayle says that one lesson he learned from watching the unraveling of the Watergate cover-up in the Nixon White House is that "when a crisis comes up, instead of covering up, get it all out. Don't go having to change your damn story, and don't let it dribble out. I mean, that's the way I operate."

That is not, however, how Quayle operated during the biggest crisis in his political life—during the firestorm of press criticism immediately after his selection as George Bush's running mate in August 1988.

Partly because of his failure to be forthright, partly because of the sloppiness of some of the early reporting and partly because of attempts by political opponents to discredit him, Quayle's reputation suffered lasting damage.

Quayle was accurately portrayed as a member of a well-to-do, prominent family, who coasted through college with mediocre grades and used family connections to make contact with Indiana National Guard officials so he could go on to law school and avoid the draft, which was sending other young men to Vietnam.

But some serious charges made against Quayle—including allegations of academic failure or dishonesty and manipulation of National Guard rules—as well as descriptions of vast wealth, appear to be false, according to scores of interviews and documents examined during the last six months.

"The thing that really makes me mad about this is because it's me," Quayle said recently, explaining his refusal to release his DePauw University and Indiana University-Indianapolis Law School transcripts. "I mean, you're not going to ask anybody else to do this. . . . This is one of the things that just makes me mad. And every once in a while when you get mad, you get stubborn."

Questions about his academic record have dogged Quayle since he entered the national political arena. When he was chosen to be Bush's running mate, professors were quoted as calling him "as vapid a student as I can recall" or "crashingly mediocre." In the sympathetic view of Sen. Richard G. Lugar (R-Ind.), Quayle's friend and former colleague, the opening days of the 1988 campaign left the public "not sure how intelligent he really is."

In December 1991, after *The Washington Post* made a renewed request for his grades, and Quayle discussed the matter with his senior staff, he telephoned to say he had reviewed his academic transcripts and would summarize them, but would not release them or allow a reporter to view them.

He said that at DePauw his "cumulative grade average was 2.16, a C. At law school, it was 2.74, a B minus." There were no failing grades, Quayle said, but he received two D's at DePauw and one D in law school. He declined to specify the courses in which he had received the low grades, and turned down an opportunity to say how many A's he had received.

"I had one course that I dropped at DePauw," he said. "My recollection isn't exact. I presume that I dropped it because I wasn't keeping up. Just a regular withdrawal, no notation of any problem. I think I was a sophomore."

"I should have done better, wish I'd done better," Quayle said after summarizing his record. Asked why he had decided not to release the transcripts, Quayle said: "I just don't want to go any further. It's irrelevant and rather demeaning."

At Quayle's request, the president of DePauw and the dean of the IU-Indianapolis Law School confirmed the accuracy of Quayle's recollections of his academic record.

More damaging than reports of a poor academic record, however, were published allegations of plagiarism. Extensive reporting uncovered no evidence that this charge or any allegations of academic dishonesty were true.

The trail of the allegations was circular, beginning with Democratic Party operatives and staff members of former Democratic senator Birch Bayh, whom Quayle had defeated in 1980. They acknowledged they told inquiring journalists in 1988 of "rumors" about Quayle and directed reporters toward certain professors for more information.

Two former DePauw professors, William L. Morrow and Michael Lawrence, were cited in particular as holding the keys to Quayle's academic past.

Contacted at the College of William and Mary, where he teaches, Morrow said, "I wish I had something on Quayle, but I don't." There were several incidents of plagiarism at DePauw during Quayle's time there, he said, and "it seemed to me one was Quayle, but I have to say, I don't know it was Quayle. . . . In 1980, the Bayh people wanted me to say he committed plagiarism and of course I couldn't."

Lawrence was reached in Santa Fe, New Mexico, where he runs an art gallery. "Every time Dan Quayle runs for public office I get called," he said. "I know of no such incident in my class or any other. To my knowledge, Dan Quayle never committed plagiarism. . . . I saw no records showing plagiarism, grade changes or undue influence in any way, shape or form."

"The amount of misinformation on this subject is so overwhelming," Lawrence added. "There is a small group of people who are hoping that wishing will make it true . . . who have made these rumors a minor career. Everyone is willing to think the worst of people on the other side of the political equation."

CALLING HOME AND ENLISTING

Stories that Quayle had used family influence and connections to enlist in the Indiana National Guard in 1969 to avoid being drafted for Vietnam thrived during the 1988 campaign in part because Quayle mishandled the issue and his answers to reporters' questions suggested he was uncomfortable with his own service.

Asked about his National Guard enlistment at a news conference the day after he was named as Bush's running mate, Quayle said: "I did not know in 1969 that I would be in this room today, I'll confess"—suggesting he was embarrassed or did something wrong. When NBC's Tom Brokaw asked that evening how he got into the Guard, Quayle said vaguely, "Phone calls were made." When CBS's Dan Rather asked whether someone in Quayle's family had called to get Quayle a spot, he replied, "I'm almost certain the governor or lieutenant governor were not involved in that"—leaving open the possibility that other high officials might have been.

Two days later, Quayle made the situation worse when he said, "Like any 22-year-old college senior, when you are thinking about making a major decision in your life . . . and whether you are going to join the National Guard . . . you call home"—suggesting at least an insensitivity to the issue of his family's prominence and influence.

Though Quayle said he favored the Vietnam War effort, he said that by 1969 he had grown disillusioned with U.S.

strategy. That year, 9,272 Americans were killed or died from injuries and 32,940 were seriously wounded in the war, and 8,553 Hoosiers were drafted. In order to go to law school, Quayle chose to enter the National Guard, which required only six months' active duty and made remote the possibility of going to Vietnam.

The circumstances of his enlistment in the Guard were somewhat out of the ordinary. Rather than simply walking in the door and asking to sign up, he and his family arranged for introductory telephone calls to senior Guard officials. But there is no indication the influence went beyond that, that he obtained admission to a unit that did not have vacancies or was placed ahead of anyone on a waiting list.

The unit he joined, the Headquarters and Headquarters Detachment (HHD) in Indianapolis, had an authorized strength of 63, according to Indiana Guard Form TDA NGW8AVAAOO dated April 1, 1969. The DA Form 1, the so-called morning report, for the unit's training assembly on Saturday and Sunday, May 17–18, 1969, shows that 52 men were serving at the time, or 11 short of authorized strength.

Quayle enlisted in the unit the next day, May 19, 1969, as an E-1 private, the lowest pay grade in the military. The morning report for the next monthly training session in June shows assigned enlisted strength at 55, or still eight short of capacity.

"There was no waiting list for HHD [Quayle's unit] before, at the time, or following his enlistment," said

Robert T. Fischer, a retired colonel and the Indiana Guard's military history project director, in a signed statement to *The Washington Post.*

As best can be pieced together now, this sequence of events led to Quayle's enlistment in the unit: As he neared graduation from DePauw, Quayle, who already had taken a pre-induction physical exam, talked to his parents about enlisting in the National Guard, so he could go on to law school. They passed word of his interest in joining the Guard to his maternal uncle, Eugene S. Pulliam, then assistant publisher of the *Indianapolis News.* Pulliam in turn visited the newspaper's managing editor, Wendell C. Phillippi, a former commanding general of the Guard, on Quayle's behalf.

Phillippi told Pulliam to send Quayle in, and after their conversation, Phillippi called then-colonel Alfred F. Ahner to tell him a good recruit would be coming over. "I did this routinely for anyone who came to see me," Phillippi said recently.

Ahner told *The Post,* "I received a number of phone calls over the years from Phillippi. . . . We always asked our commanders and former commanders" to refer potential recruits. Ahner said he checked to make sure there were vacancies in the Guard. He distinctly remembers that there were openings.

Although in 1988 Ahner was reported as saying that he "held" open a spot for Quayle, a few days later he elaborated upon his remarks—and today stands by the fuller story—insisting that no one else was denied entry because of Quayle. He said he wanted to be sure the recommended 22-year-old had a chance to interview. "I wanted to make sure they [the vacancies] didn't all go in one big blast."

In a recent interview, Quayle said he accepted partial responsibility for the way the Guard issue snowballed. His answers at the August 17, 1988, news conference, he said, did imply "that I regretted what I did. Yeah, I think that is a fair reading of the literal interpretation of it. It was not what was in my mind. What was basically in my mind was that I didn't really like the question."

Today, he is more prepared to respond to the charge of favoritism. "There just weren't any strings pulled," he said. "There were openings. . . . I don't know of anybody that applied, at least from DePauw, the group that I hung around with down there, that didn't get in."

THE FAMILY FINANCIAL PICTURE

Dan Quayle is remarkably nonchalant and uninformed about his own finances. Asked about his net worth, Quayle said recently, "I don't know," and declined to provide even the roughest estimate. "I got a house, I got a mortgage on it," he said, adding that he has some stock in Central Newspapers Inc. He is a man very uninterested in a subject that most Americans find it necessary to monitor all the time.

"I suppose a critic could say that that is a habit of people who have a lot of money," he said.

Marilyn Quayle knows much more about the family wealth. "Probably around $800,000," she said, adding, "the stock has gone down" and "our house in McLean isn't worth as much as it was."

A Price Waterhouse appraisal of the Quayles' net worth in September 1988 placed it at $859,700. The number was released publicly early in the campaign, but only after news stories had labeled Quayle the $600 million man or the $100 million man or the $50 million man. The last is the figure *Newsweek* magazine used in a story proclaiming Quayle "the wealthiest" of the four nominees on the Republican and Democratic tickets. He was probably third wealthiest of the four.

An independent examination of the Quayles' finances from public and other records indicates their principal asset is the $500,000 house they own and currently rent out, which carries a mortgage of slightly less than $150,000. They also have stock in Central Newspapers, publishers of papers in Indianapolis, Phoenix and other cities, valued at about $400,000, and several small bank accounts, investments and a retirement plan valued at more than $50,000. The newspaper stock was acquired as gifts from Quayle's family over the years.

Contrary to published assertions and speculation, Quayle does not stand to inherit part of the estate of his grandfather, Eugene C. Pulliam, who died in 1975. His grandfather did not believe in inherited wealth. Pulliam

Family Trust documents show that, at most, Quayle could receive the income from one-twelfth of the trust, but only after the death of both his step-grandmother and his mother.

At current dividend rates, Quayle would be in line to receive $76,358 a year, according to Frank E. Russell, president of Central Newspapers. That figure is confirmed by other documents.

The trust, which has nearly two-thirds of the Central Newspapers voting stock as its only asset, is irrevocable until 21 years after the death of Quayle's oldest son, Tucker, now 17, when its assets would be distributed to various heirs. Actuarial tables indicate that distribution is unlikely to take place before the year 2075.

5. *Facing Limitations in an "Awkward Job":*
Quayle as Vice President

1989–1992

Vice President Quayle (left) as he conducted a session of the National Space Council in his Old Executive Office Building quarters in November 1991. Gesturing at right is Richard H. Truly, administrator of the National Aeronautics and Space Administration, who was later fired in February 1992.

Playing volleyball while visiting troops in Saudi Arabia in 1990.

PRECEDING PAGE—Dan Quayle greets Massachusetts Republicans at a reception after a fundraising dinner in Boston in 1991.

In 1991, Vice President Dan Quayle's staff, eager for a display of heavyweight diplomacy by their boss, tried to arrange for Quayle to visit the Soviet Union. But the plans were derailed when they ran into Secretary of State James A. Baker III, President Bush's senior Cabinet official and close friend of 35 years.

Baker did not think the trip would be helpful, according to an authoritative source, and recommended to the White House against it. Baker also had recommended that Quayle not make a proposed trip to Germany during that country's unification negotiations, arguing that the vice president did not belong in the middle of the sensitive talks.

Neither trip was made. Quayle acknowledged in interviews that his staff ran into problems with the State Department over the Soviet trip, but, choosing his words with care, he insisted that there was no showdown between him and Baker. "I never suggested to the president or to the secretary of state directly that I go to the Soviet Union," he emphasized in a November 1991 interview. "I never personally brought that up."

But it was made clear by a number of sources that the secretary of state does not want Quayle to be a major player in the formulation or implementation of foreign policy.

When he travels abroad, Quayle is received as a virtual head of state. But although he has visited 42 countries as vice president, his diplomatic efforts have been restricted mainly to areas of the world on which Baker rarely focuses, such as Latin America. Quayle did visit Eastern Europe in June 1991, but as vice president he has barely set foot in the Middle East, the Persian Gulf region or Western Europe and has never been to China.

Quayle's uneasy relationship with Baker illustrates the paradoxical nature of the vice president's job. He has a privileged seat—as close as anyone to the center of power. Yet because he has no territory that is strictly his own, he can operate only in the margins of most important policy matters.

"The job is just awkward, an awkward job," Quayle said in a more reflective moment. He said he was "much more free and independent" during his eight years as senator than he is now. The vice presidency, he said, is a "much more confining job. You don't have your own agenda. Your agenda is the president's agenda."

"It's an uncomfortable position to be in," agreed Defense Secretary Richard B. Cheney. "The vice president is there sort of as an overall generalist. . . . He's here as the president's understudy, in a sense."

Operating in the president's shadow, Quayle also must tiptoe around Baker and other Cabinet members. "Wherever I might go, somebody has primary jurisdiction, and that's one of the problems with being vice president," he said. "Anything you do, you're going to be getting into somebody else's domain."

Yet while Quayle bemoans the limitations of his office, he sometimes seems unwilling or unable to follow through on those initiatives he calls his own. In August 1991, for example, he sharply criticized the legal profession and called for civil justice reform, saying there were too many lawyers making too much money from too much unnecessary litigation. But he has not taken all the steps that he acknowledged are crucial to implement the reforms.

And although he works hard, his schedule often is dominated by photo opportunities and ceremonial appearances, leading some associates to worry that he enjoys busywork at the expense of substance.

Quayle said that he and Bush have agreed on six "constituencies" that he should serve as vice president:

- The president. Quayle is both policy adviser and public spokesman, as well as an emissary representing Bush when necessary.
- Congress. As a former senator and representative, Quayle is a natural liaison for the administration.
- The Republican Party. Quayle has traveled to more than 200 cities, raising $22 million for the GOP and its candidates.

- Foreign countries. Quayle at times has played a significant if subordinate role in those accounts allowed him by the State Department—particularly in Latin America and Japan.
- The White House Council on Competitiveness. Newly active under Quayle, it oversees the writing of rules and regulations to implement legislation.
- The National Space Council. Quayle chairs this Cabinet-level group, which coordinates policy for civilian and NASA space programs.

But one item on the list clearly takes precedence over the others. "The constituency of the president is the one area you're most interested in," Quayle told *The Washington Post* in June 1991, "and that's an area I have to protect."

A PRESCRIPTION FOR THE JOB

Six years into his own vice presidency, George Bush in 1987 laid out a prescription for the job he called "the most misunderstood elective office in our political system. People either make too little or too much of it," Bush wrote in his autobiography, *Looking Forward.* Those who thought the vice president was a "useless appendage" were as mistaken as those who thought he could be a "surrogate president."

The essential attributes, Bush wrote, were subordination, loyalty and total confidentiality. "On the day a disgruntled, self-serving vice president declares civil war on the White House by publicly challenging a president, our system of government will be in serious trouble."

By this standard, Quayle gets high marks, for he has fomented no mutiny.

Only once, a senior Quayle aide said, has the vice president been cautioned about public dissent. In 1989, as Bush was flying home from his Malta summit with Soviet president Mikhail Gorbachev, Quayle told a *Washington Post* reporter that he doubted whether the Soviet Union had really given up its expansionary aims. Bush passed word that Quayle ought to let the president be the first to interpret Soviet policy. There apparently have been no further episodes of Quayle getting out of line.

Administration officials suggested that Quayle would have pressed Congress harder at the end of 1991 for legislation to spur the economy, and during the last year would have shifted support sooner than Bush and Baker did from Gorbachev to Boris Yeltsin and the republics of the then Soviet Union. But none of these disagreements was made public.

Quayle's secrecy about his advice to Bush makes it hard for outsiders to gauge his effectiveness in that role. "I like to give him my ideas in privacy," Quayle said. "When we're in a large group where it's probably going to get out, I try to be somewhat circumspect. . . . I try not to take time at large Cabinet meetings. I try to be somewhat judicious so people can't read it that the vice president feels this way, but the president feels that way."

Former vice president Walter F. Mondale agreed in a recent interview that for a vice president, "the dumbest thing to do is to go around and brag" about his influence on the president.

According to senior administration officials, Quayle influences Bush most effectively when he can take soundings within the circle of presidential advisers, find common ground with some of them and then use that alliance to advance a position. Originally an outsider in an administration dominated by people such as Baker, who had long-standing relationships with Bush, Quayle now is seen as someone who gives useful advice, as long as it is generally in line with the direction in which Bush already is headed.

"Quayle can have an impact on the tactical picture, on the domestic political and congressional maneuvering, but not on the overall strategic goals," one White House official said.

In late November 1991, for example, as the congressional session drew to a close, the White House appeared to walk away from an anti-recession tax package proposed by House Republicans. But the next day, after Quayle urged the president to close ranks with them in a show of party unity, Bush told reporters he "enthusiastically" agreed with the proposals.

In the end, however, Bush's comments turned out to be only a gesture, because he did not press Congress to remain in session to act on the package.

One of the president's closest advisers pointed out that "Bush is not easily persuaded by anyone. He will defer on details to others. . . . People, including Quayle, do move into a category where he defers to their judgment, but again only on details."

Although Quayle said, "I try not just to hang around the Oval Office, because I don't think that serves him," the most important part of Quayle's day is the time he spends with the president. Each morning at 8:15 when he and Bush are in town, Quayle joins Bush, national security adviser Brent Scowcroft and CIA briefers for about a half hour for the presidential national security briefing. After that, Quayle remains for Bush's meeting with the chief of staff for another 30 minutes. "It sets the agenda for the rest of the day," Quayle said, adding that if there is a domestic issues update, the time with Bush may extend to 10 A.M.

His proximity to the president, on a daily basis and in crisis meetings, has had a cumulative effect on their relationship, administration officials said. "You can't underestimate the slow, water-faucet-dripping impact of the [private] Thursday lunches" Bush and Quayle have each week, said the close Bush adviser. "Quayle's influence cannot be measured by a single event, but in my judgment [during the three years] . . . there has been a very definite favorable accumulation" of influence with Bush.

NATIONAL SECURITY "ODD MAN OUT"

Despite this accumulation of influence, on national security matters Quayle remains a second-team player in Washington. "I can bring certain facts and things to the table that are important to [Bush], but he has so many resources on foreign policy and he is so steeped in foreign policy himself" that the contribution is often marginal, Quayle acknowledged. One former aide called Quayle the "odd man out" among the "big eight" national security advisers because he alone has no clearly defined foreign policy role.

During the Persian Gulf crisis, Quayle became a public spokesman for the administration. On November 29, 1990, Quayle gave a speech at Seton Hall University that meticulously explained why U.S. interests in the Middle East— from the moral to the practical—warranted the risk of war. The speech, which was crafted by Quayle and his staff but cleared by Scowcroft's office, is cited by Quayle aides as an instance when he helped shape policy, and in fact its themes became the basis of some of Bush's own later statements on the crisis.

But some of Quayle's much-publicized participation in the top echelon of decision-making during the crisis was more show than substance. Much fanfare and picture-taking attended a visit by Quayle and several of his top aides to the Pentagon for a military briefing on the situation in Iraq, Saudi Arabia and Kuwait on December 17, 1990. But participants in the meeting said there was no real reason for the special briefing, which basically was arranged as a public relations display to show that the vice president was involved in the crisis deliberations.

Quayle also has received credit in the news media for urging Bush to seek congressional authorization for the use of force to drive Saddam Hussein's troops from Kuwait.

But in the internal administration debates, Quayle had urged that Bush seek the resolution before Christmas of 1990—and lost. Bush finally made the request of Congress several weeks later—in early January 1991—and it passed just days before the war began.

In June 1991, Quayle spent five days in Eastern Europe, preaching the administration line of "trade, not aid" to the heads of state of Bulgaria, Czechoslovakia, Hungary and Poland. Upon returning to Washington, he urged Bush, in a two-page memo on June 11, to relax trade barriers on the importation of Eastern European cheese, steel and textiles.

Though the administration did relax the quotas, the move was largely symbolic and had little economic impact. "I should have expanded a little bit beyond trade," Quayle said, acknowledging in retrospect that the results were "mushy."

Quayle aides said he is determined that his trips have concrete results, even if they are only announcements of routine grants. But they complained he often becomes captive of what one called State Department "ceremonialists" who tie up the vice president—sometimes with his approval—with a mind-numbing schedule of wreath-layings and routine appointments.

On June 6 during that trip, for example, after a long morning tour of Auschwitz and Birkenau concentration camps in Poland, Quayle flew to Prague, where he held a 20-minute private meeting with Czechoslovak president Vaclav Havel. Several aides complained that by acceding to the State Department schedule, Quayle missed an opportunity to have a serious discussion with one of the more important intellectual figures of recent political history. "He does not pay enough attention to his own education," said one aide.

Quayle's eight trips to Latin America have received the most notice, although there, too, he operates under State Department and White House National Security Council staff policy guidance. To the surprise of many, when he traveled to El Salvador two weeks after he was sworn in, he delivered a harsh warning on human rights abuses to the military high command and officer corps.

He called for "respect for human rights and social justice," according to a classified cable summarizing his remarks, and described himself as a "hard-liner" on human rights. "Violence must be condemned whether it comes from the left or right," he said.

Quayle recalled recently that the military did not expect such a message from someone with his right-wing reputation. "I said if I'm going to go there, let's not have it as a hand-holding session. . . . I was trying to figure out the biggest impact we could make."

Probably his most concrete achievements have come during three visits to Japan. According to White House and State Department specialists, Quayle helped persuade the Japanese to direct hundreds of millions of dollars of their foreign aid budget to countries that are U.S. policy priorities, such as Poland and Colombia. He also is credited with playing a significant role in persuading Japanese auto makers to buy billions of dollars more of American automobile parts each year.

"LEGISLATIVE COUNSELOR"

While Quayle's preferred area of operation is world affairs, his more natural home is Congress, where, as a former member of both the House and Senate, he keeps in close contact with a wide range of Republicans and Democrats. White House aides described him as a kind of "legislative counselor" to Bush. By most accounts, he is more active in this field, and more influential, than Bush was as vice president.

Congressional relations often have to do with maintaining friendships and creating an atmosphere, and both are Quayle specialties. According to three dozen legislators interviewed from both parties, Quayle leaves them with the impression that they have a direct channel to the White House through him.

When his travel schedule does not take him out of town, Quayle goes up to Capitol Hill at midday on Tuesday and Wednesday and spends the rest of the afternoon working his old turf.

On Tuesdays at noon, he usually attends the weekly luncheon of Republican senators. Often, Quayle leads off the session with comments on his recent travels or a plug for an administration program or nominee. After lunch, Quayle frequently crosses the Capitol to attend the weekly House Republican strategy session in the office of Minority Leader Robert H. Michel (Ill.). And on Wednesdays, he often goes to the informal lunches of one of the other major groups of Senate Republicans—the conservative Steering Committee or the moderate Wednesday Group.

Quayle belonged to both as a senator and works hard at maintaining his ties across the GOP spectrum.

Sen. Richard G. Lugar, a leader of the Wednesday Group, said that "when Dan comes in here, he just takes whatever seat is open; if it's in the back row, he'll slide in with a plate of food. It's just as if he were a member of the club, getting his three minutes to talk about whatever subject he wants to talk about."

Quayle clearly enjoys the informal chats with old friends, and he brings back a personal assessment of the legislative climate that is valued in the White House. According to former White House chief of staff John H. Sununu, Quayle's "social contacts" on the Hill have been "invaluable." He said Quayle's vote-count estimates "turned out to be very right" in the unsuccessful fight to confirm John G. Tower as defense secretary at the outset of the administration, and have carried weight ever since. "When we lay out a legislative strategy, almost automatically he's a key part of the discussions," Sununu said before his resignation.

Defense Secretary Cheney said that Quayle "probably has better ties at any given moment, or a better read on . . . the mood of the Senate Republicans—and the Senate generally—than just about anybody else."

These judgments come from friends, of course, but Quayle clearly is useful on Capitol Hill. Knowing the importance of having respected senators undertake a personal cause, he was the first White House official to call Sens. John C. Danforth (R-Mo.) and Sam Nunn (D-Ga.) about supporting Judge Clarence Thomas's nomination to the Supreme Court, and he has lobbied on both sides of the aisle on almost every major issue.

Sen. Malcolm Wallop (Wyo.), chairman of the Steering Committee, a caucus of about 20 conservative Republicans, said the vice president served as the broker between that group and the administration on a 1989 minimum wage bill and succeeded in heading off the threat of a conservative filibuster. He enlisted conservative support for the president's veto of technology restrictions relating to the FSX, a fighter plane that was to be developed in conjunction with Japan. "Quayle was the one who persuaded a very reluctant Steering Committee to go along," Wallop said.

But during the 1990 budget battle, when conservatives revolted against the agreement between Bush and congressional Democrats, Quayle was hard-pressed. Senate Minority Leader Robert J. Dole (R-Kan.) said, "Dan made calls, particularly to the Steering Committee group and the more conservative members, trying to help the president. He's been good at that." But even his own successor from Indiana in the Senate, Dan Coats, would not be swayed. "I told him early on I was going to vote exactly the way he would have voted if he were still the senator from Indiana," Coats said. "He didn't put a lot of pressure on me."

In that same fight, after Bush reneged on his "no-new-taxes" campaign pledge, House Minority Whip Newt Gingrich (R-Ga.) recalled recently, "there was a period where we were not talking with [budget director Richard G.] Darman and Sununu. For three or four days, Quayle was the primary source of information between the most active wing of the House Republican Party and the White House. . . . And he did so without breaking his ties in either direction."

101

"He didn't come to us and say, 'You guys are really right,' " Gingrich added, even though it was well known to the conservatives that Quayle had opposed the budget deal in private White House discussions. But at a time when Sununu was threatening political retaliation against Republicans who broke with the president, Quayle played the peacemaker, Gingrich said. "He came to us and said, 'Look, I'm with the president. You guys are being jerks. But you are *our* jerks.' He kept a lot of additional brawls from going on."

Quayle also keeps private channels of communication open with some liberal Democrats. Early in 1991, one Democratic senator said, Quayle told him that a compromise was possible on a family-leave bill that had been vetoed by Bush the previous year. The senator said he was advised by Quayle, "Don't let that bill come up [early] this year," when Bush would feel politically obligated to threaten another veto. Later in 1991, he quoted Quayle as saying, Bush might be more receptive to "a substantive discussion" of the issue.

The advice to delay action on family-leave legislation until late last year was taken, and friends of Quayle, both Republicans and Democrats, later put together a compromise proposal. But contrary to what Quayle had hinted, Bush remained adamantly opposed to it.

When asked about the matter recently, Quayle reacted as if he had been caught with his hand in the cookie jar. "Golly, don't get me involved in this thing publicly," he pleaded. "The president's position right now is not to support that legislation."

FREQUENT POLITICAL EXCURSIONS

On the Republican political circuit, Quayle is almost constantly in demand. He makes a political trip somewhere around the country at least once or twice a week, usually returning the same night.

Quayle's job is to touch the dozens of reelection bases that Bush does not have time to visit. "Although Bush probably does more [political speeches] than any other president," Quayle said, "he can't be consumed by it. We can. We can do an awful lot."

These daylong excursions, for which local party organizations contribute from $8,000 to $15,000 in partial reimbursement of the travel costs, are jampacked. Quayle may leave early enough to give both a breakfast and lunch speech, and usually one at dinner as well. Crammed in between are pep talks to state party organizations, meetings with local newspaper editorial boards, brief news conferences, closed-door sessions with local business leaders or other interest groups and a sprinkling of photo opportunities.

The party faithful show up with checkbooks: Generally it's $50 for a lunch ticket, $150 to $200 for a reception and $1,000 to participate in a round-table discussion with Quayle and several dozen other big donors. Often, too, Quayle will squeeze in a round of hand-shaking at a supermarket, a fast-food restaurant or a bowling alley, a nostalgic return to the press-the-flesh campaigning at which he excelled in Indiana.

Typical of many such excursions on which *The Post* accompanied Quayle in 1991 was an 11-hour day trip to Chicago last summer to address the American Medical Association and meet with a group of 35 Polish-American leaders, followed by a stop in Philadelphia to meet with Cardinal John Krol and speak at two GOP fund-raisers. In the AMA speech he praised doctors, criticized lawyers and was generally well received.

Veterans Affairs Secretary Edward J. Derwinski, who earlier in his career had advised Vice President Bush on dealings with ethnic organizations, came along at Quayle's request to critique his performance before the Polish group.

At that midday session, Quayle talked nonstop for 10 minutes, reviewing his recent trip to Eastern Europe, noting that he had met with Polish president Lech Walesa, and praising the Polish leader for his courage, his sense of humor and his "wonderful wife." He fielded two questions.

The reception was less enthusiastic than at other stops during the day, and Derwinski was critical, privately telling Quayle afterward that he seemed to be overcompensating for his perceived faults and trying to prove, among other things, that he knew how to pronounce the names of the Polish prime minister and economic minister. Quayle had not played enough to the politics of the situation, Derwinski said, comparing him to President Bush, who, in a similar meeting with a group of ethnic leaders, talked for just a few minutes and then went around the table, looking each leader in the eye and asking open-ended questions that gave them a chance to speak their minds.

Edward Moskal, president of the Polish group in Chicago, said later that Quayle did not seem to have an in-depth grasp of the situation in Poland and had talked down to them. "Frankly, we weren't impressed," Moskal said.

During his performance in Philadelphia later that evening, Quayle seemed more comfortable, offering the partisan crowd a stock speech bashing the Democrats with bumper-sticker slogans. With a bright, confident smile, Quayle proclaimed the Republicans the party of "strong defense, lower taxes, a strong economy and no quotas" and called the Democrats "empty on new ideas."

"We've been thrilled by him," Chris Bravacos, political director of the Pennsylvania Republican Committee, said afterward. "Our chairman [Anne B. Anstine] has a whole wall filled with pictures of the vice president. He's been very good to us."

Even in Washington, Quayle's days often end with fund-raising receptions for Republican officeholders. He displays remarkable patience with picture-taking, frequently standing for an hour as one donor after another is hustled by for a handshake, smile and photo.

Quayle's staff calls it "flash for cash."

LACKING THE FOLLOW-UP

Quayle's preoccupation with the ritual and protocol of his office often sidetracks his big projects.

Before launching his civil justice reform initiative in an August 1991 speech to the American Bar Association, Quayle said in an interview that it would be a "shot across the bow" of the legal system.

More than 50 detailed proposals—limiting punitive damage awards, the use of expert testimony and the cost and duration of the pretrial "discovery" process; experimenting with a "loser-pays" rule; and offering alternatives to litigation—were developed by Solicitor General Kenneth W. Starr, then cleared and approved by Quayle's Council on Competitiveness. When Quayle unveiled them to the ABA, he salted the specifics with rhetorical passages questioning whether "America really needs 70 percent of the world's lawyers . . . and 18 million new lawsuits a year."

But since then, Quayle has found only a handful of occasions for follow-up speeches. While Bush has issued an executive order carrying out some of the proposals, the promised recommendations for action by Congress and model legislation for the states have not yet been forthcoming.

In the interview, just before the initiative was made public, Quayle volunteered that "I've got to sit down with Joe Biden [the Democratic chairman of the Senate Judiciary Committee] sometime just to see how interested he is" in cooperating.

Yet nearly four months later, as Congress was preparing to adjourn for the year, Quayle said he had not gotten around to seeing Biden. "I do need to do that. . . . I should have sat down with him and talked about it. . . ."

6. *The Vice President's Driving Passion: Quayle Unleashes Competitive Energy on the Golf Course*

Running with Marilyn Quayle, son Benjamin and daughter Corinne in a benefit race in 1990 to raise money for research, diagnosis and treatment of breast cancer.

Quayle, second from left, was captain of the 1969 golf team at DePauw University and its top player.

PRECEDING PAGE—(Left) Shooting hoops with his son Tucker in 1989. (Right) Quayle showed his golf form in June 1991 in a professional/amateur match in Memphis.

At 5:50 A.M. on Friday, July 12, 1991, Vice President Dan Quayle, four aides and seven Secret Service agents departed the vice president's residence by helicopter for the 10-minute ride to Andrews Air Force Base.

It was the beginning of an 18-hour day that would take Quayle on Air Force Two to New York for a speech at the Waldorf-Astoria Hotel, an editorial board meeting at the *New York Post* and the opening ceremonies for a disabled athletes organization on Long Island.

He finished all this by lunchtime. Page 12 of Quayle's detailed schedule that day then listed "Washington Work/ Private Time: 6 hours." What it really meant was golf.

From time to time, aides and political advisers have urged Quayle to cut back on his golf, telling him that it reinforces an image of the elite, carefree child of privilege. But Quayle has refused, so his staff has learned to build his passion into their planning. They schedule important meetings, interviews and events several hours before he is to leave for the course. "He goes on a high," one aide says. But the event cannot be too close to the game, because then Quayle will be distracted by his desire to get to the course to practice before teeing off.

Golf has been a major part of Dan Quayle's life since his youth in Arizona, where the family lived next to the Paradise Valley Golf Club. His grandfather, Eugene C. Pulliam, once told him that the golf course was a good place to make "contacts and business acquaintances."

But golf serves a special function for Quayle now that he is in the vice presidency, an office where he can never forget that he is, as former vice president Nelson A. Rockefeller put it, "standby equipment," and where he can never fully unleash his competitive energies.

David Griffiths, a golf buddy from law school days, said: "One of the things people don't understand about him is how fierce a competitor he is. Even when we were playing head-to-head, just the two of us, it was still very competitive." When Quayle fell behind, "invariably, he'd come roaring back."

Quayle's onetime aide and his successor in the Senate, Dan Coats, has a reputation as one of the toughest competitors on Capitol Hill, but he said he was no match for Quayle. "He hates to lose. All politicians are competitive, but most do not have the intensity that Dan does. . . . The key to understanding Dan, competing against him and working with him—the tougher it gets, the more determined he is."

AN EIGHT-HOUR MARATHON

The intensity of his urge to excel was demonstrated that July 12 during what turned into an eight-hour golf marathon at Deepdale Golf Club in Manhasset, Long Island.

By 1:15 P.M. Quayle, in blue trousers and a pink shirt, was on the veranda of Deepdale—one of the most exclusive and expensive private clubs in the country. He and four others—Rep. Raymond J. McGrath (R-N.Y.), real estate developer Lewis Rudin, club professional Darrell Kestner and George Zahringer, a stockbroker and one of the best amateur golfers in the nation—had the lush, beautifully manicured course virtually to themselves.

Quayle began the outing with 30 minutes on the driving range, trying new clubs while Kestner diagnosed his swing. His drives are the best part of his game, carrying 250 to 275 yards, but Quayle was far from satisfied.

As he headed out to the 6,623-yard course, teams of Secret Service agents, and the military aide carrying the "football" with the nuclear war codes (who travels regularly with Quayle), fanned out in separate golf carts, communicating with hand-held radios. "SCORECARD is 150 yards from the green," said one agent, using Quayle's code name. Caddies drove the golf carts with the clubs; Quayle walked. One caddie acted as a ball spotter, while another taped Quayle's shots on a portable Sony video camera.

Quayle told pro Kestner and amateur Zahringer to

111

advise him freely but not to overload the circuits with too many tips and criticisms. During the first nine holes, reviewing his performance on the video, they focused on three areas: keeping the shoulders down, proper location of the knees on the backswing and keeping the shaft of the club vertical on the top portion of the backswing.

On the 397-yard, par-4 14th hole, Quayle hit what looked like a perfect drive, only to see it take a radical departure to the left, hooking deep into the woods. The spotter located it in a thicket of tall, thin trees.

Quayle spent a full minute, utterly calm, trying to develop a strategy for recovery. He saw the only way out was back toward the tee, against all golfing instinct to advance toward the hole. A lofted shot into the middle of the fairway provided a nice shot to the green. But the recovery was incomplete, because he sliced the next shot to the right. He ended up with a double bogey 6 on the hole.

On the 431-yard, par-4 15th, Quayle sliced his drive to the right into an adjacent fairway, and had to shoot over a line of trees to get to the green. On the 18th, he putted out for a final score of 81, 11 over par. It was not what he had hoped for, and his face showed it. Club pro Kestner shot a 72, amateur Zahringer a 67.

Golf is key to understanding the vice president, said one of his closest aides. "It's the personality that goes with being a world-class golfer. You know, they're not the people who wrap their clubs around the trees. They are not the people who shout at the galleries. They are not the people who let their bad performance on the first hole affect their performance on the sixth hole. And while they're playing the sixth hole, they are not thinking about the 18th hole. . . . It helps me understand why he doesn't go through each day thinking about how this is going to affect the California primary in 1996."

A group of Quayle's aides waited at the edge of the green, including Dan Murphy, who carried an official-looking suitcase and a canvas bag, both filled with what Quayle's staff called "chum"—meaning bait—an assortment of Dan Quayle memorabilia including tie bars, T-shirts, golf balls and visors. As Lewis Rudin distributed crisp $100 bills to the caddies and ball spotter, the other golfers went into a mild "chum" feeding frenzy, nearly emptying Murphy's bags.

Murphy, who has since left Quayle's staff for law school, said there are two things about his job he would not miss: carrying the "chum" all over the country and the world, and picking up Quayle's clothing in various hotel rooms and residences.

DRIVING INTO THE NIGHT

Though he was scheduled to depart the club in about 15 minutes, Quayle headed to the driving range. For the next hour and 50 minutes, he hit balls as Kestner and Zahringer analyzed problems with his swing. As the sun set, Quayle continued to pound ball after ball down the range, achieving a nice zing with most shots, finding his groove, sending the balls regularly 250 yards or more.

"Mr. Vice President," one of his coaches finally said, "the sun is down. No one has been able to even remotely see where the last half-dozen shots landed."

Quayle seemed to come out of a trance. "We'll take a shower, then get something to eat," he said. Afterward, his skin was pink and his blue eyes stood out even more than usual; he looked younger; he seemed totally relaxed.

Over thick steaks and baked potatoes, accompanied by a 1982 Chateau Margaux wine, the talk was all of golf. Quayle launched a round of nostalgia, recalling with exactitude incidents from a 1966 tournament in San Francisco where he helped set the pins, and a 1975 tournament at Medinah Country Club in Illinois, where he and his wife, Marilyn, saw pro Ben Crenshaw hit his shot in the water on the 17th hole.

About 9:30, Quayle was ready to leave. With cleared freeways, Air Force Two and a waiting Marine Two helicopter, he was home by 11:30.

People who know Quayle emphasize his eagerness for the game and its importance to his psychic balance. During his round at Deepdale, he had exclaimed, "I can't get enough of it!"

He likes to play at Burning Tree in Bethesda, where normally he can finish in two-thirds the time it would take at other local courses, and where his "Honorary Resident" membership exempts him from joining or paying the initiation fee. One Secret Service agent said that there are summer weeks when Quayle plays as many as three or four times.

He had a putting green built at the vice presidential residence. "After an evening appearance that did not go as well as he wanted, and he was clearly not happy with his performance," one aide said, "I have seen him, in the dark of night, jump out of his car and walk right to the putting green and start putting. The imposition of discipline. Or absolute order. What matters. And that's not just relaxation. That's his version of Oriental shadow-boxing."

Marilyn Quayle said of her husband's love of golf: "If you're going to play a good game of golf, everything else has to leave. . . . It requires such a level of concentration that everything that's closing in on you and pounding you . . . it's total relief."

7. *Quayles and Bushes,*
Almost Like Family

After George Bush announced that Dan Quayle was his choice of running mate, Quayle repeatedly grasped Bush by the arm and shoulders and cried out to the crowd: "Let's go get 'em! All right? You got it?" News coverage compared him to a game-show contestant who had just won the Oldsmobile. It was the first of the awkward campaign moments that would give him a reputation as a lightweight.

Originally an outsider in an administration dominated by people with long-standing ties to Bush, Quayle, here lunching with the president, has worked hard to become accepted. His counsel is now considered useful, as long as it is generally in line with the direction in which Bush is already headed.

Riding through the streets of West Carrollton, Ohio, at the end of the first difficult week of the 1988 campaign, Dan Quayle recalled in a recent interview, he and Marilyn shared a lighthearted mood with George and Barbara Bush.

The couples were playing what they called "the limousine game," competing to see who could make eye contact with the most roadside spectators. If one of them succeeded in making direct contact with a voter, even for just a fleeting second, even at a hundred feet, they assumed, that voter would be a supporter for life.

The four cheered and jeered each other, laughter cascading all around. "He [Bush] is very good at it, much better than I," Quayle said. "Eye contact. You have to have eye contact."

The Bushes and the Quayles had known each other for 10 years before they became political partners, but it was the 1988 campaign that sealed their friendship.

Bush had campaigned for Quayle in both 1978 and 1980. In 1985, Quayle brought the then vice president to Fort Wayne, Indiana, for a fund-raiser to help intimidate the city's Democratic mayor, a potential challenger to Quayle's 1986 Senate reelection who ultimately did not run. Two insiders who observed the Bushes and Quayles together at an event for Quayle's 1986 race said the couples got along extremely well, as if they were family.

Both Bush and Quayle possess "a good, perverse sense of humor . . . an almost irreverent humor," said John H. Sununu, Bush's first presidential chief of staff.

Marilyn Quayle said that the informal tone Bush sets in the White House fits perfectly with her husband's nature. People casually "pop in and out of each other's offices," she said, "because the president does. He comes down, even checks on the furniture in Dan's office to see what's been changed. It's really funny, he's so cute."

Despite the 23-year difference in their ages, friends say, the two men are remarkably alike, down to their love of sports and their limitations on the dance floor. White House Chief of Staff Samuel K. Skinner said he thinks Bush picked Quayle as his running mate because he "likes the way he deals with people. George Bush does not like to have people on his team who are petty, who are cheap-shot artists. He wants . . . people who think of others. And Dan Quayle fits that category."

"Both of them are very decent human beings," Marilyn Quayle said. "Neither of them is ugly to others."

Bush's grandchildren play with, and sometimes stay over at the home of, the Quayle children, and Quayle's son Benjamin, 15, has become a regular guest at Camp David with Bush's grandson George P. Bush, also 15.

Bush and Quayle also share an appetite for political trivia. Quayle vacuums his staff for items of political interest before each weekly lunch with the president. "As a former national chairman, he [Bush] enjoys the tidbits [about] what the state chairmen are doing and what they're not doing," Quayle said recently, adding that he is often "amazed [that] he will already know it. . . . I tell him, 'You don't need me. You already know all this.' "

Beyond that, Bush has thrown a protective blanket around Quayle. Sen. Alan K. Simpson (R-Wyo.), a close friend of both men, recalled that during the early months of the administration, when Quayle was the butt of widespread humor, "The greatest thing George told him— I don't know when it was—but he said, 'What do you think of all those cartoons and editorials and attacks?' and Dan said, 'Wow!' and just shook his head.

"And George said, 'Well, why don't you take [out] the word "Quayle" and insert the word "Bush" wherever it appears, and that's the crap I took for eight years. Wimp. Sycophant. Lapdog. Poop. Lightweight. Boob. Squirrel. Asshole. George Bush.'

"That meant more to Dan, I think, than anything," Simpson said.

When Simpson's comments were repeated to Quayle recently, he placed the conversation in the first half of 1989. He laughingly suggested that the language sounded more like Simpson than Bush, but confirmed that he was touched by the president's solicitude.

8. The Competitiveness Council:
Curbing Federal Rules, Leaving "No Fingerprints"

Some of Quayle's participation in decision-making during the Persian Gulf crisis was more show than substance; participants say that his visit to the Pentagon for a briefing in December 1990 was basically a public relations display.

PRECEDING PAGE—*After his election to the Senate in 1980, Dan Quayle prepares to move from his House of Representatives office.*

Vice President Dan Quayle, a self-proclaimed "zealot when it comes to deregulation," has made his chairmanship of the President's Council on Competitiveness a command post for a war against government regulation of American business.

Democratic members of Congress, public interest groups, environmentalists and others have attacked the council for intervening in behalf of business to scuttle regulations that are the direct responsibility of other federal agencies. Seven congressional committees are investigating the council's activities. But the council's real role is much larger than even its critics imagine.

A six-month examination of the council's work by *The Washington Post* shows that Quayle and his small council staff of free-market activists have intervened in dozens of unpublicized controversies over important federal regulations, leaving what vice presidential aides call "no finger-prints" on the results of its interventions.

They have changed or tried to change regulations on federal rules relating to commercial aircraft noise, bank liability on property loans, housing accessibility for the disabled, clothing makers' right to work at home, disclosure requirements on pensions, protection of underground water from landfill runoff, reporting requirements for child-care facilities located in religious institutions and fees for real estate settlements.

"The future of the country is at stake," Quayle said in an interview, "because if you can't figure out a way to basically tame that bureaucracy, and if we can't do it on our watch . . . then who's going to do it? . . . The bureaucrats are smart, they've been here, they've got more ways to skin a cat than you can think of, [and] they've got the press primarily on their side."

Quayle said he has broad authority from President Bush to step into the process of writing federal regulations—the thousands of rules published each year to implement laws passed by Congress—wherever he deems necessary. "I am doing what the president wants me to do," he said of what has become his most substantive vice presidential role. "That is to make sure that 'regulatory creep'—to use his words—does not get back into his administration."

The council's power is enhanced by what several officials described as an unwritten administration rule that no Cabinet official will appeal its actions to Bush. "I'm the last stop before the president," Quayle said. "I have not had a decision appealed from the Competitiveness Council to the president."

The new White House chief of staff, Samuel K. Skinner, described a "gentlemen's agreement" among administration officials to avoid asking Bush to resolve any disputes except those of utmost importance.

"Why bother the president if you don't have to?" Skinner said in a 1991 interview while he was still serving as transportation secretary. "Number one, you might lose. . . . Number two, you're burdening him with something that he does not like to be burdened with. He wants people to work it out. The gentlemen's agreement is try to work it out before it gets to him." Bush, according to Skinner, says, " 'I don't want to have to decide between Cabinet members.' Everybody understands that's what the president wants. . . . Anybody that's loyal to the president is going to do it that way."

Together, the "no fingerprints" and "no appeal" rules make Dan Quayle the man to see in the Bush administration for business people across the country and their Washington lobbyists.

Richard Rahn, until recently chief economist of the U.S. Chamber of Commerce, said: "Quayle has gotten into the deregulation battle more substantively than anyone else. He has done his homework. He's forceful. And he's made a difference in the eyes of American business."

In the process, Quayle has infuriated critics such as Rep. Henry A. Waxman (D-Calif.), chairman of the House

Energy and Commerce subcommittee on health and the environment, who has accused Quayle of setting up "an illegal shadow government." In an interview, Waxman compared what he called Quayle's "rogue operation" on the domestic front to the Reagan administration's secret maneuvers uncovered in the Iran-contra investigations. "The Council on Competitiveness has usurped power, holds secret meetings with industry groups, and violates administrative procedures on public hearings and public access to information on decision-making," Waxman said.

Waxman said he has long suspected that Quayle and the council staff are involved in many more behind-the-scenes activities, but congressional investigations have been able to bring only a few of the actions to light.

By attempting to "rewrite the laws through regulations" that are so technical "that the public cannot understand," Waxman said, "Quayle has set out to make himself the hero of the conservative forces in this country." Unless there is a public outcry, he said, "it's going to be difficult to stop him," because the issues of the council's authority and its interpretations of the law will take years to resolve in federal courts.

Quayle defended all of the council's actions as proper and legal. He called the criticism "good, old-fashioned politics," and a testament to the council's effectiveness in reducing regulations favored by Democrats.

ALTERING AN ESTABLISHED PROCESS

Generally considered a flexible and adaptable politician, Quayle reserves his most passionate political denunciations for "regulatory creep."

As a senator, he kept on his office wall a framed copy of an editorial that his grandfather Pulliam wrote in 1971. The title, "Will the Federal Bureaucracy Destroy Individual Freedom in America?," is one that Quayle quotes often.

In his work with the council, as in other aspects of the vice presidency, Quayle has built on the model George Bush established during his eight years in the job. Bush chaired a similar group, called the Task Force on Regulatory Relief, and its annual reports bragged of reducing regulations, liberating free-market forces and getting the bureaucracy off the backs of Americans.

C. Boyden Gray, now Bush's White House counsel, managed the project for non-lawyer Bush and opened the regulatory process to business voices.

A Reagan administration executive order authorized the Office of Management and Budget (OMB) to review regulations for cost effectiveness before agencies make them final. Frequently, there are bitter disputes between the departments and OMB, or between two agencies, over the strictness with which new laws should be applied. In addition, the members of the Democratic-controlled Congress who wrote the bills often want the most rigid interpretations applied, while a business-oriented, Republican administration wants to make the regulatory burden as light as possible.

By putting Quayle and the Competitiveness Council into the game as a kind of Supreme Court of regulations, Bush has altered a well-established federal regulatory process, sanctioned by law, that allows all interested parties the opportunity to comment publicly and argue their positions on the record before regulations are issued. The change has lessened the rule-making power of federal agencies and tipped the outcome of these battles against those in Congress who push for strict regulation.

The council consists of seven members: Quayle, the White House chief of staff, the attorney general, the director of OMB, the chairman of the Council of Economic Advisers and the secretaries of treasury and commerce. Meetings of the full council are rare, and most of the work is done informally by Quayle and his staff. Quayle said this is intentional.

"I'd much rather have the collision below, rather than . . . at the Competitiveness Council," where stories of bureaucratic battles are more likely to leak because more people are involved, Quayle said. "In this town, especially, you don't want that to come out, that you [did] not prevail. Everybody's a winner—as long as it doesn't get out."

The council was relatively inactive until mid-1990, when Bush and the business community perceived backsliding from the Reagan administration's deregulatory victories. Directly charged by the president to address the issue more actively, Quayle hired Allan B. Hubbard as the council's executive director. A graduate of both Harvard law and business schools, and the multimillionaire part owner of an Indiana chemical company, Hubbard had managed former Delaware governor Pierre S. "Pete" du Pont IV's bid for the 1988 presidential nomination. Hubbard's wife, Kathy, had been Quayle's chief fund-raiser in his 1980 Senate campaign.

Like others in the libertarian wing of the Republican Party, Hubbard is a strong believer in the efficiency of the free market. "We want to make sure the regulations are consistent with the statutes," he said in an interview. "But we also want to be sure they are the least burdensome to the economy, to protect American competitiveness and preserve American jobs."

As his deputy, Hubbard selected another ardent advocate of free-market economics, David M. McIntosh, a 1983 graduate of the University of Chicago law school and alumnus of the Justice Department.

"Hubbard and McIntosh are the driving force" at the council, said one White House official. Quayle said he encourages and fully supports their conservative activism.

One of Hubbard's first moves as executive director was to ask OMB's Office of Information and Regulatory Affairs for a list of issues on which the agencies had been dragging their feet.

Hubbard and McIntosh began applying the heat to agency lawyers in phone calls or meetings to resolve these issues. Hubbard met personally with the number-two officials in many agencies and departments, calling on Quayle to talk to the appropriate Cabinet secretaries when Hubbard was not satisfied.

Word quickly spread through the business community that the Competitiveness Council was ready and able to help on regulatory matters, and its agenda filled up.

In almost every city he visits as a campaigner, Quayle holds closed-door round tables with businesspeople who have made sizable contributions to the local or national GOP. Hubbard, who also has the title of deputy vice presidential chief of staff, often travels with Quayle and sits in on these sessions.

BREAK FOR AIRLINES, NOT FOR EARS

On July 8, 1991, Sen. Wendell H. Ford (D-Ky.), chairman of the Commerce, Science and Transportation subcommittee on aviation, and an author of the 1990 Airport Noise and Capacity Act, wrote to Quayle asking for help. United Parcel Service, which has a major facility in Kentucky, and several commercial airlines had complained to Ford that a proposed Federal Aviation Administration (FAA) rule implementing part of the legislation would unnecessarily hurt them financially and put them at a competitive disadvantage with foreign carriers.

The act requires U.S. airlines to replace noisy aircraft with new, quieter jets by the year 2000. The proposed FAA regulation spread the timetable for getting rid of the noisy planes at a steady pace over the next 10 years, with 25 percent of them to be phased out by 1994, 50 percent by 1996, and 75 percent by 1998.

The airlines had argued to the FAA and OMB, without success, that the rules should emphasize "phasing in," not "phasing out," thereby giving them credit for the quieter planes they had already purchased and allowing them to retain noisy jets in the fleet for years longer.

Ford insisted that the FAA's proposal was far more stringent than Congress had intended. And while the solution proposed by the airlines would mean prolonged noise for millions who live near airports, it also would provide a tremendous economic break at a time of airline bankruptcies and mergers. According to one analysis used by the council, the airlines' proposal would save the industry $1.2 billion.

Quayle took up the matter directly with Skinner, then the secretary of transportation, the post that oversees the FAA. The two midwesterners are golfing buddies, having played together several dozen times in the last three years.

"I talked with Sam periodically" about the aircraft issue, Quayle said, asking, " 'How's it going?' "

Meanwhile, Hubbard convened a dozen meetings with officials of the FAA, Transportation Department and OMB, seeking an agreement. Hubbard's threat of direct intervention by Quayle and the council ultimately convinced the FAA that a relaxation of the timetable would still comply with the law, and the industry proposal was accepted in its entirety.

"We do not have a monopoly on good ideas," said Kenneth P. Quinn, the FAA's chief counsel. "We welcomed the input of the Competitiveness Council. We learned something . . . and the final rule was a reasonable balancing of environmental benefits versus the economic costs."

Quinn said he had close to 100 conversations or meetings with Skinner over the year they were considering the issue, and although the Competitiveness Council, OMB and the Council of Economic Advisers were heavily involved, "the secretary's prerogative to decide the issue was legitimately preserved" and Skinner "himself made the decision."

It was Skinner who announced the decision, on September 24. It attracted heavy news coverage, for it involved the economic plans of 30 airlines with 2,000 planes and a delay in relieving the eardrums of 3 million people who live near noisy airport flight paths.

Patrick J. Russell, an attorney for the National Airport Watch Group, which represents 300 local anti-noise groups in 75 cities, complained that citizens had little input in a ruling that directly affected them. A *USA Today* editorial said Skinner's message to those who live near airports was: "Things will be better in 10 years. Meanwhile stuff it. Uncle Sam knows what's best."

News stories barely mentioned the role played by the Competitiveness Council—and that was just as Quayle wanted it. His staff had discussed the possibility of publicizing his part in the decision and decided not to, because they recognized it was a "political loser," as one of Quayle's aides said. "Millions of people hate airplane noise, and there was no benefit to be derived from being associated with the decision that would mean more noise longer," the aide said.

DISPUTE ON DEFINING WETLANDS

"We've had sometimes more visibility than I really want," Quayle said of the publicity surrounding the council. He said he would prefer that most of their interventions, like that on aircraft noise, leave no fingerprints.

But at the same time, Quayle and the president derive immense political benefit from business and big-donor Republican circles because of the council's deregulatory activities.

How many issues has the council been involved in? "Whew, quite a few," Quayle said. "I don't have a number, but this is a big government and people know our mandate is to hold down regulations and try to follow the deregulatory effort that the president established when he was vice president."

Other officials said that Quayle and the council staff limit the interventions to about 50 cases a year, tending to choose those with major economic impact. While Hubbard and McIntosh handle the detailed negotiations with the agencies, Quayle's chief of staff, William Kristol, keeps OMB director Richard G. Darman, presidential domestic policy adviser Roger Porter and the White House chief of staff advised of council activities.

It is the use of informal, back channels outside public or congressional purview—designed partly to thwart publicity and partly to hold down the temperature of disputes within the government—that critics say denies the protections of open government. The approach is illustrated in the case of regulations governing development of the nation's wetlands.

During the 1988 presidential campaign, Bush focused the spotlight on wetlands, pledging "no net loss" of these ecologically fragile areas that foster wildlife and birds, help control floods and filter out contaminants before they enter streams.

Immediately after the election, but before Bush took office, technical specialists at the Environmental Protection Agency (EPA) and three other agencies issued a manual more strictly defining wetlands in a way that expanded development restrictions on tens of millions of acres.

On his political swings around the country, Quayle said, he heard frequent complaints that the federal government was unnecessarily restricting the use of wetlands for real estate development and other business ventures. Ohio governor George Voinovich (R), for whom Quayle had campaigned extensively, "jumped all over me," Quayle recalled, "about one airport expansion project in northwest Ohio" that was being delayed by the wetlands restrictions.

In May 1991, an official said, Quayle told the council's executive director: "Hubbard, we need to do something about wetlands." EPA administrator William K. Reilly protested against the intervention. Some White House officials argued that the hot-potato issue should be left to EPA and the other agencies, but Quayle received Bush's approval to become involved.

During the summer, negotiations hit innumerable snags. On the night before Reilly was to testify to the Senate, he, Quayle and Hubbard engaged in a round-robin series of telephone conversations trying to broker a deal. Each time Reilly thought he had Quayle's agreement, Hubbard called Reilly to say he had misunderstood. When their final agreement was presented at a White House senior staff meeting the next morning, Darman and Chief of Staff Sununu erupted, and a last-minute call was made to Reilly—in his car on the way to the hearing—to tell him the deal was off.

After that near fiasco, Quayle convened the full Competitiveness Council on July 29. He began the session by expressing astonishment that vast areas of his home state of Indiana could have been classified as wetlands under the original definition in the manual, when he knew those areas were farmland.

According to those present, it quickly became clear that most of the agencies wanted to open more wetlands to development than Reilly did. But Quayle did not let the matter come to a vote, nor did he announce his own decision. "Didn't want to do it," he said in a recent interview. "Too many people spoke up and I felt that we needed a little cooling-off period to see if we could work this out."

Quayle aides suggested that the vice president was being protective of Reilly, knowing that a formal vote overruling the EPA chief's position would leak to the press and damage Reilly with environmental organizations and EPA professionals.

The opportunity for further negotiation came the next day, when Reilly came to Quayle's office to discuss matters related to the vice president's upcoming trip to Latin America. At the end of the visit, Quayle and Hubbard broached a compromise that had surfaced the previous day. The meeting ended without conclusion, but Quayle sent Hubbard after Reilly to press for an answer. Standing near his car in the driveway between the White House and the Old Executive Office Building, Reilly said he'd think about it overnight. The next day he phoned Hubbard to say yes.

The eventual announcement of the deal, which significantly narrowed the definition of wetlands in a way experts have said would halve the amount of protected acreage, served only to stoke the controversy. Final rules remain under review. Environmental groups have assailed the decision, but Quayle said Republican leaders in states such as Georgia and Louisiana have told him that "the best thing you've done is to stop EPA taking away people's property rights." Rep. Waxman has vowed that "at some point, Reilly is going to be called to face how far he is letting this go."

Quayle insisted that he and Reilly are not antagonists. "We have a very good understanding," Quayle said. "He comes at these issues from a very strong environmental point of view, [and] I argue there's some other things that need to be considered." Reilly, who reportedly blames Sununu for many of his problems, apparently harbors no grudge against Quayle. He has told associates that he does not think the council "compromised the integrity of the regulatory process. We are in a process of give and take."

But the critics are likely to press a procedural issue that troubles even some senior administration officials—the question whether such informal sessions as the Reilly-Hubbard-Quayle meeting violate the rules of open advocacy that govern the regulatory process.

One senior regulatory official, who asked not to be named, said, "I believe in public notice and public comment, and it is not a good idea to have Vice President Quayle and his staff skewing that process."

This official and two senior officials in other agencies said that it was embarrassing that Quayle and his staff could have conversations with businesspeople and others on regulatory matters and not have to report them on the public docket. Said one official of what is standard agency practice, "My people are under strict instructions not to talk to regulated parties, and if they meet someone at a cocktail party and have a discussion inadvertently they must write a memo and file it" with the public record.

In December 1991, Waxman and others raised conflict-of-interest allegations against Hubbard, who responded by pledging to put his substantial wealth in a blind trust. Waxman, however, is not satisfied and says that Quayle himself should have a blind trust. Quayle has nearly $400,000 of stock in Central Newspapers Inc., which is affected by trash recycling regulations the council has handled.

"I don't think they [Quayle and Hubbard] are motivated by traditional greed," Waxman said. "But the attitude is inconsistent with the standards set by Bush for his administration, which is supposed to be [that] there will be no appearance of a conflict."

Quayle rejected that view. "We are trying to hash out differences within the administration," he said, "and this is a rather normal White House function. . . . Congress doesn't like the White House meddling, period. They feel that EPA, for example, should be more beholden to the

139

Congress than to the executive branch. Well, that's just the normal tension that you have between the legislative and the executive branch. We're just diametrically opposed. The White House should be concerned and involved on a rather detailed basis on what kind of regulations are out there. We get blamed for them."

Quayle promised that the deregulation crusade would go forward, and held two long meetings with his staff before Christmas to draw up a list of regulations and issues the council plans to target in 1992.

RECENT CASES OF COUNCIL INTERVENTION

Here are some recent cases from the "no fingerprints" file of the Council on Competitiveness. Confirmed by Vice President Quayle, these council actions involve regulations that already have been issued or that are pending:

• Ensuring that the Labor Department plans to lift a ban on work done at home by workers in the women's clothing industry, a move long opposed by the International Ladies Garment Workers Union: Quayle said he has spoken with Labor Secretary Lynn Martin and "my understanding is that they are preparing the [new] rule." A senior administration official said that Quayle and Martin are still discussing the issue, and Martin has made no final decision.

- Easing of regulations drafted by the Environmental Protection Agency (EPA) that would require expensive liners and water runoff systems to be installed at municipal landfills for non-hazardous waste.

- Backing the OMB in a dispute with the Pension and Welfare Benefits Administration (PWBA) over investment options for pension plan beneficiaries: OMB argued that a proposed rule would increase administrative costs for small pension plans and also might reduce returns for investors. The final rule, in accordance with OMB wishes, limited the investment choices and the frequency with which beneficiaries could transfer their money among them.

- Backing OMB in another dispute with PWBA over the disclosure of information to pension plan beneficiaries: PWBA had outlined specific procedures that pension providers had to follow to alert beneficiaries of news about their plans. The final rule supported OMB's move to trim those procedures.

- Easing Department of Housing and Urban Development (HUD) regulations, opposed by OMB, that pertain to the Fair Housing Amendments Act of 1988: HUD proposed that all apartment buildings covered under the act meet certain standards for accessibility to the handicapped. The new regulations allow an apartment owner to wait until a disabled person rents an individual unit to bring it up to standards.

- Mediating between the Labor Department and the Immigration and Naturalization Service over whether the 400,000 foreign students working in this country must be paid the prevailing wage: It was agreed to treat them like American students, who can sometimes be paid less.
- Settling a dispute between the Treasury Department and EPA over whether banks could be held responsible for hazardous waste cleanup on property on which they had made loans: The final agreement minimized the banks' liability.
- Easing regulations, proposed by the Department of Health and Human Services, that would have required child-care facilities based in churches and other religious institutions to report extensively on their activities to the government.
- Intervening on the side of OMB in a dispute with HUD over regulations implementing the Real Estate Settlement and Procedures Act: The council told HUD it disapproved of a rule prohibiting the use of certain computerized loan origination systems that are profitable to businesses; HUD is expected to modify the rule soon to allow for some exceptions to the ban.

9. *The Space Council:*
Debating NASA's Future

At a Bush/Quayle '92 general reception, Quayle talks with Rep. Dick` Nichols (R–Kansas) in the Wistin Crowne Center, Kansas City, Missouri.

At a meeting with automotive industry representatives in Detroit, Quayle conducted a round-table discussion to explore ideas regarding rejuvenating the auto industry.

I n the summer of 1990, after the failure of the Hubble orbiting telescope and repeated delays in space shuttle launches had seriously embarrassed the National Aeronautics and Space Administration (NASA), Vice President Quayle had a rare chance to demonstrate his abilities as an executive. Space was Quayle's bailiwick. Soon after their inauguration in 1989, President Bush had named him chairman of the National Space Council, with responsibility for coordinating the government's space-related activities.

Quayle asked for recommendations on what to do about NASA's problems. Mark J. Albrecht, whom he had appointed executive secretary of the Space Council, handed him a blunt memo on July 10, 1990. In it Albrecht offered two options.

The first, he wrote, was to "BLAME THE CONGRESS" for squeezing NASA's budget. The second was to "BLAME THE

BUREAUCRACY: A large and hide-bound bureaucracy at NASA has consistently put self-preservation above program excellence. . . ." At NASA, Albrecht wrote, " 'Cover Your Ass' substitutes for 'Get it Right.' "

Quayle chose option two, and convened a 12-member panel of former politicians and space experts to review NASA's future. It was chaired by Norman R. Augustine, chief executive of Martin Marietta Corp. The principal subject before the Augustine commission, as the panel became known, was whether to give priority to space exploration or science projects.

Exploration—particularly the celebrated manned missions to the moon—has brought the space program popular support and inspired national pride. It is also something Bush has enthusiastically supported. In a speech the summer of 1989, the president pledged a "long-range, continuing commitment" to space exploration, and asked his Space Council to draw up a plan for orbiting a space station, establishing a base on the moon and sending astronauts around Mars.

But many space scientists have argued that robotic science missions, which involve complicated research but lack appeal to the layman, have given humankind its greatest wealth of useful knowledge. The Augustine panel had to weigh these conflicting positions.

By Tuesday, December 4, 1990, the Augustine commission had largely finished its work and gathered at the vice president's residence for what was supposed to have been a celebratory dinner but became a working session that hammered out the report's conclusions. Also present were Albrecht, NASA administrator Richard H. Truly and Richard G. Darman, head of the OMB and a space enthusiast.

A DELICATE SITUATION

Accounts of that evening, taken from the notes of several participants and interviews with 14 of the 16 who attended, provide a revealing glimpse of Quayle's mode of operation in a delicate situation.

Over soup, Quayle thanked the group and cautioned against leaks to the news media. Augustine then explained that, while the report was not to be released until the following Monday, he had arranged through NASA for it to be distributed on Capitol Hill on Friday—in just three days—because several key legislators were going home for the weekend.

A hush fell over the table.

According to one commission member's notes of the dinner, Quayle had been "counting on releasing [the report himself] to upgrade his public image. Should we give out copies to notoriously leaky legislative staffers three days before the executive branch sees it? Had we forgotten our responsibility to make the boss look good?"

This note-taker's account continued: "The worried Vice President kicked this one around with Norm [Augustine] for about 15 minutes. . . . We decided to confine the Friday meeting to members only (no staffers), warn attendees to maintain secrecy, give out as little paper as possible, state that attendance was being taken and hope for the best over the weekend. The soup course was delicious, but our working session was off to a lousy start."

Quayle then asked what exciting projects the commission was going to propose that he could enthusiastically support, reminding his guests that he would be helping to sell it to the administration, Congress and the public.

Augustine said they had ranked five space endeavors in order of priority. Number one, he said, was science.

Science? Quayle asked, looking puzzled. Could they be specific?

Louis J. Lanzerotti, an AT&T scientist and NASA investigator, launched into an impassioned discourse on how science was the fundamental building block for comprehension of the environment, education of future scientists, improvement of the quality of life and the survival of the human race.

Quayle leaned over to commission vice chairman and planetary scientist Laurel L. Wilkening, she recalled in an interview, and said, "Here we go again. This is kind of fun."

Quayle listened intently. According to Lanzerotti, Quayle "kept probing and questioning . . . trying to understand. . . . I thought the vice president was businesslike and thoughtful in getting to the bottom of our thinking."

But Darman, according to Lanzerotti and others at the dinner, was growing uncomfortable, and was furiously taking notes.

"A pained vice president asked what was our second priority," according to the written account of a participant.

Technology, said Augustine, noting the importance of the electronics and engines that made all space missions possible. There was silence. The study of Earth's climate and environment, Augustine said, came third.

"Darman groaned," recalled Wilkening and others.

Augustine then hurried to priority four: a new launch vehicle to replace the $5 billion-a-year space shuttle. Fifth and last was the manned mission to Mars and the space station—top priorities in Bush's speech the previous year.

Darman lectured the group on how budget priorities worked. Listing something last, he said, was an invitation to kill it. Did the commission on the future of the U.S. space program really want to proclaim to Congress, the American public and the world that space exploration was so unimportant that it could be scrapped?

Darman said later in an interview that while it would have been improper for him or Quayle to impose his opinions on the commission, he did feel a need to note how its priorities were "inconsistent" with stated administration policy.

"I remember we had to rework it," Quayle recalled, "and Darman was very pivotal in this."

"Darman raised the issue of prioritization," remembered Augustine. "Nobody was giving us instructions . . . but [he said] to be very aware of the hazards of preparing the whole space program in priority order."

As Darman continued to hammer hard on the priority listing over dessert and coffee, the commission members agreed to recast their report. Science would still be priority one, but the report would speak of a balanced program and all the other subjects would be lumped together, abandoning any priority listing.

According to the notes of one participant and to three others, Darman's farewell to Quayle was, "Thank you for a fine dinner, Dan. Good thing I came. I saved your damn report."

Asked about this recently, Quayle recalled, laughing, "I vaguely remember that."

ABANDON THE STATION?

The final Augustine report read like a compromise document. Despite the report's attempt to play down the top priority assigned to science, news accounts reported it as the commission's central conclusion. For the administration, the toughest question in implementing the report was the future of the space station, which Bush had so warmly endorsed in 1989. Quayle made it clear to his aides that he wanted to assert leadership and make a bold proposal in response to the Augustine recommendations.

Some of Quayle's aides—notably his chief of staff, William Kristol, and his national security adviser, Carnes Lord—recommended killing the space station, a position widely endorsed in the scientific community. Killing the station would be a dramatic move, his aides said, not only on its merits but as a way to show that Quayle, and not Darman or Truly, was in charge.

Albrecht prepared a memo for Quayle outlining the arguments against the space station: It cost too much, and its estimated 1997 launch date would yield no "concrete accomplishments in space" during Bush's tenure as president.

But Darman, a strong backer of the station, argued that abandoning it would set back space exploration for years. He told Quayle that if it was not funded, the money would wind up going to domestic social programs, not to space. And cancellation would be an enormous public relations setback.

On March 14, 1991, Quayle and Darman met for a half hour. Quayle emerged a supporter of the station—and last summer successfully fought to restore its funding after a House committee moved to scrap it. Darman gave Quayle credit for "an important decision. . . . [The] station would not be here if he had decided otherwise."

In a recent interview, Quayle denied suggestions by some administration officials that he "got rolled" by Darman. "He didn't roll me because I knew what the arguments were," he said. "I'm not rolled. People present me the facts and I make up my mind." He said he agreed that cancellation would be a public relations disaster.

Summing up the episode, Quayle said, "We've tried to be rather bold, rather aggressive. And when you do that, you're bound to break some furniture." But on reflection, he added, "Maybe I'll even say that we haven't broken enough."

Quayle finally saw to the breaking of a large piece of furniture at NASA. Despite having thrown his weight behind the space station, he felt that the NASA bureaucracy was still too hidebound, self-protective and unresponsive to changing technologies and budget realities. Quayle argued to Bush that the problem started at the top and that he wanted NASA Administrator Truly out. In February 1992, in a gesture highly uncharacteristic of his presidency, Bush fired Truly.

10. Marilyn Quayle: Guardian of the Quayle Image

(Left) Mrs. Quayle talks to youngsters at an unscheduled stop at a mall in Kansas City.

(Below) Marilyn Quayle blows a kiss to a friend in the audience at a fund-raising event in the Copley Plaza Hotel in Boston.

(Below) At an inaugural ball, the Quayles celebrate their political success.

PRECEDING PAGE—*(Above) The Quayle family celebrates at Republican headquarters in Indianapolis after Dan Quayle's election to the Senate in 1980. (Below) Marilyn Quayle conducting a meeting in her office regarding the International Disaster Advisory Committee, which she chairs.*

B y the spring of 1989, about four months after Dan Quayle took office as vice president, reports were so widespread that his wife, Marilyn, was the dominant, smarter partner in the Quayle twosome that she banished herself from her husband's new offices in both the White House West Wing and the Old Executive Office Building next door.

"I can't help him now," she told a longtime friend over lunch. Marilyn Quayle, the friend said, "was at her wits' end" as news accounts continued to portray Quayle as not up to the job. "Her husband was being pounded into the ground and she knew she had to back away. . . . The more she helped, the worse it got."

Marilyn Quayle recalled, "It became apparent that enough of a myth had been drawn up that it was detrimental." The myth, she said, was that she "ran the campaign because Dan was too weak" or that she was some sort of "magic manipulator" of her husband. All untrue, "unfair and ridiculous," she said. "It was frustrating, very frustrating because . . . Dan and I were used to operating in a certain way."

Since their marriage in 1972, through his campaigns and terms in the House and Senate, and during the 1988 vice presidential race, they always had operated as a team. Immersed in his career, she approved all campaign brochures, pictures, newsletters and commercials. She received daily packets containing his schedule, legislative calendars, drafts of proposed legislation and staff memos.

Her exile from his offices lasted only until attention shifted away. By early 1991, she had moved into a six-office suite in the Old Executive Office Building—twice the size of the one occupied by Barbara Bush when she was Second Lady—just across the hall from the vice presidential office. The proximity makes for more involvement, she said. The Quayles talk "three or four times a day," and always have. "Our relationship is such that if I want to get ahold of him for anything, I'll call him and right then. . . . He had them put in a drop line so that he can just push a button and he's got me if I'm in my office . . . as I will do with him."

Once again, she said, she is her husband's "eyes and ears" with his staff and his chief political adviser.

Marilyn Tucker Quayle, 42, described herself as part of a new generation of political spouses who have "a professional role as opposed to kind of backdoor."

It is not necessarily the profession she would have chosen, and part of her story is of the frustrations of an intelligent woman who has abandoned the legal career for which she trained, and which she deeply wanted, and taken a back seat to the ambitions of the man she married.

But it is a role she has thrown herself into wholeheart-edly—at times in a way that has infuriated those she has encountered along the way. One of Dan Quayle's close associates calls her the "hard half" of the Quayle partner-ship. Political colleagues of her husband's described their surprise, and sometimes pained amusement, at her level of involvement as his more disciplined, professional alter ego. Stories of her angry outbursts and intimidation of others are sufficiently widespread that she has divided his staff over whether she is an asset or a liability to him.

From interviews with Marilyn Quayle and a number of her closest friends, as well as with Dan Quayle and associ-ates of one or both of them, a portrait emerges of a com-plicated, bright, strong-willed woman who demands perfection of herself and others. Many agree that if he ever became president, she could be the most influential First Lady in American history.

While Dan Quayle's style is marked by informality— "radiant nice-guyism," in the words of one of his associ-ates—Marilyn Quayle has a definite imperious side. Those who are in her favor praise her generosity and warmth. But many who have come into contact with her say they have found it a chilling experience. There have been a number of incidents, verified for this report, in which Dan Quayle associates or staff members—senior and junior—felt snubbed or belittled by Marilyn Quayle.

One Navy steward assigned to the vice presidential residence was sufficiently concerned about his future after he
refused to iron the family's clothing—a task that Barbara
Bush paid extra to have done when she was Second Lady—
that he wrote to President Bush to make sure his career
was not damaged. Bush wrote back and reassured him.

A number of Dan Quayle's aides said they felt unwel-
come and uncomfortable in Marilyn Quayle's presence or
office. There is a palpable lightening of mood during trips
on Air Force Two when she is not along.

All this has little apparent effect on Dan Quayle, according to even Marilyn Quayle's severest critics. When they fly
together on Air Force Two, the Quayles spend hours talking alone to each other; in Washington, he instantly takes
every telephone call from her during the day; he expresses
approval and glee when some of her mischievous statements—such as her critical comments about James A.
Baker III, Bush's 1988 campaign manager, whom she
blames for some of the miscues that caused Quayle problems during the race—are reported to him.

During seven hours of interviews, Marilyn Quayle frequently ascribed to herself the very characteristics and
work habits that others often find lacking in Dan Quayle—
doing her homework, mastering subjects, rarely making a
public mistake.

Despite the criticism and frustration, retreat is not her
style. Her approach to her favorite recreation—horseback
riding—provides an apt metaphor. "I ride hard, I ride fast,"
she said. "There is no room for error. And if there is error,
you hurt yourself very bad."

"ALWAYS A SERIOUS PERSON"

Marilyn and Dan Quayle married after they had dated for 10 weeks while students at Indiana University Law School in 1972. The daughter of two southern Indiana physicians, she described herself as "always a serious person," who was given music, dancing and horseback riding lessons, and was expected to do well in school. "I was rather rebellious and decided early on that I would be a lawyer instead of a doctor, but there was no question that I would . . . be something professional."

For two years they shared offices in Huntington, Indiana, while he worked at his father's newspaper and she practiced law. Over the next 12 years, she played major roles in his political campaigns and the offices he held—representative (1977–81) and senator (1981–89)—and raised their three children.

She was determined that her position and influence continue after his election as vice president.

Two days after the inauguration in 1989, she tackled head-on what she felt was one of the most important tasks her husband faced in taking over from George Bush. From 1985 to 1988, while Quayle had been senator from Indiana and Bush had been vice president, Bush's Capitol office had been run by his longtime personal aide Jennifer Fitzgerald, who had a reputation for guarding the premises—and access to Bush—with fierce protectiveness.

Marilyn Quayle knew that her gregarious husband—eager to be Bush's representative on the Hill and the administration's top lobbyist—wanted and needed to see many more people in his congressional office. "She said she very much wanted it to be a . . . working office, accessible, open, serviceable," said William J. Gribbin, Vice President Quayle's congressional liaison chief.

Furniture was rearranged, new desks and extra phones were installed, and staff members were instructed to make it comfortable and easy for White House and departmental lobbyists, senators and their aides to feel they could hold informal meetings there, get their work done and nurture their links to the vice president.

"It was obvious this was not a congressional spouse off on her own," Gribbin recalled. "I realized after that first meeting that what I had on my hands was a tremendous asset—somebody who knew this business as well as I did, or better, and came in here knowing exactly what kind of adjustments had to be made."

The signs of her influence show up in large and small ways. Because of her interest in cancer detection and treatment—one of the causes she has championed as Second Lady—the President's Council on Competitiveness, which Dan Quayle chairs, sent out a letter over his signature requesting a study of cancer's economic costs. Quayle's staff said she made suggestions about the civil justice reform effort and attack on the legal establishment that he launched in the summer of 1991, and she comments frequently on his political agenda.

She said she believes his staff finds "an ease of coming in and discussing concerns with me, whether it's the direction things are going or whatever they don't want to bother Dan with." Staff members also check "if I think it's important enough to bring it up to Dan," she said. If it's not, "they let me make that decision instead." People in Indiana or out on the campaign trail, she says, have a "feeling of being closer if it goes through me, things they don't want to discuss with staff."

She declined to elaborate further on her role, but it is obvious that she has Dan Quayle's total confidence. "Marilyn, she knows what's going on and she has a very definite opinion about the way things should or should not happen," he said. "She has a sense of what I'm doing, and if she thinks that we ought to be doing something else, she tells me."

She said, "I still get a packet every night" of information about his schedule and substantive decisions being considered.

MAINTAINING APPEARANCES

In no role is Marilyn Quayle more dedicated than as the keeper of Dan Quayle's image. His former congressional staff members tell of trying to get a formal photograph of him back in 1977 when he was first in Congress. They kept sending proofs to her and she kept rejecting them. "She was very attuned to pictures of him and his image, and retained approval right," said one former staff member who dealt directly with her.

By 1986, when Quayle was running for reelection to the Senate, Roger Ailes, the Bush media consultant, was his official image-maker.

Ailes wanted a freeze-frame of Quayle to end the commercials he was making. "Dan had absolutely no concern" about which picture was used, recalled Ailes. "But Marilyn did." After she rejected at least 15 possibilities he had sent her, an exasperated Ailes allowed her to come to his editing studio in New York, something he said he has never permitted another non-candidate to do. Finally, they agreed on one of Quayle in an open shirt standing informally in front of some trees. But that was not the end of it.

"She thought [a] branch was coming out of his head," Ailes said, and she said it looked like antlers. "Why . . . I still don't know. . . . I never quite understood that, but she was very interested in it." Finally, Ailes's staff air-brushed out the branch.

The final product, Marilyn Quayle recalled, was "great. . . . I'm a perfectionist and [Ailes] was putting out a product and I expected it to be perfect. I was there to make sure it was done perfectly."

"I swear to God, my whole staff and I still joke about it," said Ailes. "When I see Marilyn I say, 'I saw a shot of Dan, he really looked ugly. You'd better get to work.' I still don't know what the hell she's talking about."

Her concern about her husband's image was more dramatically displayed one morning in 1991 when she visited the small suite of offices her husband maintains in the Dirksen Senate Office Building. On the wall was a large photograph of him finishing a golf swing. His shirt had gathered and filled at his stomach, suggesting a paunch.

"You can't have that up there," Marilyn Quayle said she remembers saying. "It's terrible. . . . Take it down. . . . Look at that stomach!"

Loretta Coupland, a five-year veteran of Quayle's staff, removed the 18-by-24-inch photo, pasted on thick cardboard in a wooden frame without glass, from the wall.

"That's just awful," Marilyn Quayle told Coupland and two other staff members in the office that day. She picked up a pen and began scribbling out her husband's image with deep, heavy strokes, first the midsection and then the rest of him. "I made it so you couldn't see who it was," she recalled.

At first, said one of the women who witnessed the incident, "We took it pretty much as a joke . . . but it got very intense. . . . It did flash through my mind: She's taking a lot out on that picture."

Once she had finished the scribbling, Marilyn Quayle said, it crossed her mind that she had compounded the problem. "I realized somebody could take that and . . . say, 'Oh . . . what's she been doing?'. . . . And I realized that would be bad, you know: 'The vice president's wife did that.' "

"Loretta," she said she told Coupland, "you still will hang it back up and you'll say: 'Look at what Mrs. Quayle did to that.' "

An eyewitness said that Marilyn Quayle then placed the picture on the floor and, "She kicked it."

"I do not recall kicking it," said Marilyn Quayle, "but if I did, it was to get it out of the frame, no other reason." Once the picture was dislodged from its frame, "I just peeled it off the cardboard and told Loretta to send the frame and the cardboard back here . . . so they could use it again," she said. "And I just tore it up into pieces and threw it in the wastebasket."

Her final words, all agreed, were, "I don't want to ever see this again."

In contemporaneous accounts of the incident, the three women described it to others as bizarre and troubling. In an interview, one of the eyewitnesses said, "To do it in front of all of us. I've seen some pretty goofy things, but nothing like this. . . . Human behavior is a strange thing."

Coupland said, "I don't feel at liberty to talk about that."

At least one account reached the vice president himself. Quayle said he asked his wife if she had kicked the picture. "I forget exactly what her response was," he said, "and she sort of laughed."

But the symbolic import of her actions, and the reactions of others, apparently weigh on Marilyn Quayle. In a final half-hour interview in which she spoke about the picture incident and other matters, she described it as a "lark," and a joke that had been misinterpreted.

But during the interview, she became alternately distraught and indignant over the prospect of the incident becoming public. At several points, her voice quavered and she became tearful.

"I don't lose my temper very often," she said. "I am not violent."

"PUTTING THE FEAR INTO PEOPLE"

Greg Zoeller, a former member of Quayle's Senate staff, said he had "always gotten along with Mrs. Quayle, and I . . . think I'll kind of burst the bubble of her kind of being the witch of the office.

"Around the Senate she was very clever about saying a few things at certain times that would become legend. And she does have a way of kind of putting the fear into people. It's up front. Even in the vice president's office, she's dropped a couple of things . . . the word of mouth makes them into legend that she's just crucified some poor junior staff member."

According to Zoeller, she has deliberately created a myth around herself that "she can be cruel and just cutthroat."

"It's kind of a lesson that everybody can understand. You do something that looks like it hurts the vice president, you're going to get in trouble with Mrs. Quayle," Zoeller said. "Because Dan will never get mad at anybody. He'll be disappointed, but he never gets mad."

Marilyn Quayle has, on occasion, fired members of her husband's staff, including Diane Weinstein, Quayle's first legal counsel as vice president. "She was in a position where I had good expertise and had to deal with it," Marilyn Quayle said. "And I must say the decision was treated by the rest of the staff with relief."

Dan Quayle said that his staff should not worry about his wife. "They shouldn't be intimidated. I've heard that, but they shouldn't be."

But several close associates of the vice president's, projecting his wife as a potential First Lady, made a perhaps inevitable comparison.

"I think she'd be another Nancy Reagan," said Richard Fishering, an assistant county Republican chairman in Indiana who worked closely with Marilyn Quayle on her husband's first congressional race in 1976.

"I wouldn't want her to get the idea she was president of the United States," said Orvas Beers, who has been the GOP chairman of Allen County, Indiana, for 30 years and gave Quayle his start in Indiana politics.

Said one current close Quayle associate, "If she got to be First Lady, the public would soon forget about Nancy Reagan. Nancy would soon be considered a woman of the people."

Asked directly about the comparison to Nancy Reagan, Marilyn Quayle said, "I'm definitely not a manipulator. I look at our relationship more as a collegial relationship than mommy taking care of her little boy, which is the way the press portrayed" Nancy Reagan.

The difference between the Quayles and most married couples, Dan Quayle said, is not that his wife is deeply involved in his career, but that they are willing "to acknowledge [it] up front." Asked if Bess Truman, for example, was as involved when her husband was vice president in the 1940s, Quayle said, "I imagine she had a lot to say about it. Oh I bet, you'd better bet your bottom dollar she did."

Marilyn Quayle says she agrees the difference is her husband's willingness to speak publicly about her substantive role. "He's not embarrassed to say—before, you know, your little wifey, you never admit your wife helps you. Even Barbara Bush has been in on just about everything her husband's done. Oh, yes, you're dreaming if you think she hasn't."

"I'm not going to comment on that," Dan Quayle said.

HOMEWORK AND HIGH PRAISE

"She's not a scientist, but she is a brilliant woman," Sam Broder, director of the National Cancer Institute, said of Marilyn Quayle. "I very rarely use the word 'brilliant,' but she learns, she retains, she grasps in the way a few, very brilliant people can, even in a field that is not theirs."

After the 1988 election, when she contemplated life as the nation's Second Lady, "I thought, man, it's going to be tea and crumpets and I would just go nuts," Marilyn Quayle said. She decided to apply herself to cancer detection and disaster relief, and she has become a public advocate for both. She wins exceptionally high praise from government professionals, who marvel at her seriousness and technical comprehension of the subjects.

As a promoter of early detection and prompt treatment of breast cancer—which claimed her mother's life in 1975—Marilyn Quayle "brings a great air of moral authority, credibility and clarity," Broder said. He said he has never encountered an official in Washington with a greater appetite for briefing materials, or greater skill in asking probing questions.

When Broder's comments were relayed to her, Marilyn Quayle responded with pride and relief. Her fear, she said, was that she would be regarded by such professionals as "just window dressing. . . . [I thought that] if I knew as much as I could possibly know, then I would be accepted and I could actually make a difference. And if you don't do your homework, you can't."

Similar praise came from Andrew S. Natsios, the U.S. Agency for International Development's director of foreign disaster assistance, who traveled with her to Mexico and to Bangladesh. "She has never made a mistake," Natsios said. "She always says the right thing. . . . She could do my job."

Not only does she have a technician's understanding of the legal and logistical aspects of disaster preparedness, said Wallace E. Stickney, director of the Federal Emergency Management Agency, which handles domestic disasters, "I've never seen anyone who relates better to those people" who have suffered losses.

Marilyn Quayle keeps an active daily schedule but said she agrees to speak in public only at political events, or about cancer prevention and disaster relief. "I usually speak without any notes," she said, adding that "I pretty well speak my mind." When she reads a speech, she said, "I can pick up any text you give me and can pretty well get it right the first time with the right inflection."

The same thoroughness and energy are devoted to home and family. She invested countless hours in the restoration of the vice presidential residence on Massachusetts Avenue NW, lobbying successfully with the House and Senate Appropriations subcommittees for funds to supplement private donations to pay for the renovation, and inviting some of the members to tour the home with her.

"Took them top to bottom around the house," she recalled during an interview, "and I said, 'Guys, this is wrong. You got to help me on this.' . . . We don't have handicapped bathrooms, we don't have a ramp, we don't have a lift to get them up, because the house is all stairs. . . . It's a disgrace to the country."

Today, in addition to full accessibility for the disabled, the house has new wiring, a new pool house, flagstone decking and landscaping. "It's a charming, charming home," Marilyn Quayle said. "It's really an oasis. . . . It's one of the best-kept secrets in Washington. The grounds are fabulous. You really are private here. . . . We spend most of our time out on the veranda or out by the pool."

Marilyn Quayle also has spent the last 2½ years writing a political thriller, centered on Cuba after the death of Fidel Castro, with her sister Nancy T. Northcott. Scheduled for publication in spring 1992, the 320-page book is entitled *Embrace the Serpent.*

By numerous accounts, Marilyn Quayle is a loving and attentive mother, taking time to coach a school soccer team and involving herself in the details of the lives of her three children—Tucker, 17; Benjamin, 15; and Corinne, 12. The

169

two boys attend Gonzaga College High School; Corinne is a student at the National Cathedral School for Girls.

Friends recall images of her, during Quayle's House and Senate years, in her van on the Beltway with kids packed in the back, heading to a soccer game. She made a point of being there for every school open house and play. When her children balked at eating vegetables, she got them interested by helping them start a garden in the backyard.

To the extent possible, the Quayles have tried to maintain a normal home atmosphere. Bill Neale, an old friend from Indianapolis, said that the Quayles "make a real effort to be sure that one of them, whenever possible, is there for breakfast with the kids—and hopefully both of them. They will travel late at night to get home to be there, so they can talk about what's going to go on that day, what they're doing in school, in athletics, whatever it may be. . . . They strive hard to have a typical family life. It's hard . . . but they do a pretty darn good job of it."

Marilyn Quayle has a close group of professional women friends who share her interest in sports and provide a safe haven. Once a year, they escape to what they call "camp" at a remote location for several days without their husbands. "Marilyn's core group," as one called it, includes Rae Evans, a vice president of Hallmark Cards Inc.; Eva Kasten, a senior vice president and director of the Washington office of the Advertising Council and wife of Sen. Robert W. Kasten Jr. (R-Wis.); Mary Howell, a vice president of Textron Inc.; Carol Adelman, a senior official at the Agency for International Development; Deborah

Dingell, a senior official at General Motors Inc. and wife of Rep. John D. Dingell (D-Mich.); and Sheila Tate, president of Powell Tate, a Washington-based public relations firm and press secretary to Nancy Reagan when she was First Lady.

The friendships transcend party affiliation, Marilyn Quayle said. "Among political wives there is a basic understanding . . . that we're all going through the same thing."

ADJUSTING AFTER THE 1988 ELECTION

Nineteen eighty-eight, when Dan Quayle was in the second year of his second Senate term, was supposed to be Marilyn Quayle's opportunity finally to commence her long-postponed legal career. Instead, she spent the year helping her husband catch George Bush's eye for the vice presidential nomination, then watching him be trashed on the campaign trail.

When the campaign was over, and Dan Quayle was elected vice president, she wanted to join a law firm or find a professional position for herself. Several firms were interested, she said, but financial disclosure rules requiring her to list law clients, and other political, legal and practical considerations—including a round-the-clock Secret Service presence—conspired to make it virtually impossible for the

Second Lady to take an outside job. Job offers from within federal departments and agencies also had to be declined.

Robert D. Orr, then governor of Indiana, confirmed that the Senate seat her husband vacated was hers for the asking. "It was mine if I wanted it," she said. "It was mine." But, she said, she could see that if she ever voted against the administration, she would create a "big story" that would be "hard on the president." So she said no.

She was inhibited, she recalled, not only by fear of political and legal conflicts, but by uncertainty about the time demands of being Second Lady. "The one thing I was afraid of is I would get in a position and . . . and then realize I really didn't have the time to do it. And I didn't want to be a failure. . . . That would be a bad precedent to set for anyone coming after me."

There were other adjustments as well, most notably the transformation in Dan Quayle's status. "The children and I had come to this [realization]," Marilyn Quayle said. "The vice president never can be just Dan Quayle, Dad." At sports events or traveling, "the family does have to, in public, pull aside."

The harshness of the 1988 campaign and the barriers to her own career she encountered as Second Lady came as a surprise, close friends said. "It was a roadblock that was not anticipated," said Eva Kasten. "It was not a little roadblock. It was cement."

Marilyn Quayle said she preferred to call them "yield signs here and there . . . you do keep hitting those yield signs, hitting the bends in the road." She repeatedly plays down the emotions.

Another friend said, "After the 1988 campaign, she kept it all in. I worried a little that an igloo was being erected around her and the last piece of ice would go in and she would freeze over permanently." Still another longtime friend said, "It has been a long dark journey, very, very painful."

Asked directly about these characterizations, Marilyn Quayle said, "They're not very close friends. That is definitely not my personality. I don't ever brood about anything." But the friends who are quoted were exclusively from a list provided by Marilyn Quayle herself. Pressed on the question, she said that she was "probably angry, pain not so much."

"I don't know how you resolve all these conflicts 100 percent," said Eva Kasten. "It's always there. One hundred percent is not achievable. I would put her in the 90 percent category in terms of satisfaction and self-esteem. She's not bitter. . . . Bitterness is too strong a word. It implies a hardened woman with an emotional scar. She has strength. She can get through anything that life dishes out.

"She is very black and white. She makes judgments clearly, quickly and firmly and very vocally. She is very opinionated. She has a clear vision of what she wants," Kasten said. "I wish I had more of her qualities . . . directness, commitment and passion. I've never known Dan without Marilyn because Marilyn has been so participating. It has been a political career for the family as opposed to one just for Dan Quayle."

Added Rae Evans, "Truly the worst is over. The passage out of the worst in fact has been made. I don't think there is an incident that they would find impossible to manage."

"I look at the bright side of everything," Marilyn Quayle said. "I try to find the silver lining in everything." Political wives "do have to look over [their] shoulder at everything. . . . You really do have to make opportunities for yourself and you have to go the extra mile always. Or you sit back and you're not a part of your husband's life. You have a separate life."

She added, "What has ended up is I have the best of all worlds."

11. What If Dan Quayle Were to Become President?

Quayle and Allan B. Hubbard, his deputy chief of staff and executive director of the President's Council on Competitiveness, riding on Air Force Two in December 1991 with Bernadine P. Healy, director of the National Institutes of Health.

O n Wednesday, January 8, 1992, for the second time in eight months, President Bush's sudden illness thrust this question on the nation and the world: What if Dan Quayle became president?

The 200-plus people interviewed about Quayle—people who grew up with Quayle, who served with him in Congress, who ran campaigns for and against him and who work with him in the Bush administration—agreed on several parts of the answer.

Quayle, they said, would bring to the White House a basic decency and an even-tempered disposition. As former vice president Walter F. Mondale put it, he is "Midwest nice." He also would bring an able staff, and Ronald Reagan–like conservative convictions about the evils of bureaucratic regulation and high taxes. Yet his record indicates he would be as ready to negotiate as to fight.

But even many of his friends and close associates

expressed doubts about Quayle's intellectual depth, his knowledge and understanding of history and his appreciation of the social forces that have shaped his own generation. Colleagues questioned whether he has the stature to lead the nation. His ingratiating personality has won him more affection than respect. Many Americans, according to the polls, are uncomfortable even having him as vice president.

Six months of reporting on Quayle revealed a more complex and resourceful politician than the comic-strip caricature that emerged during the 1988 campaign. But it did not dispel the impression that this former C-student is a man of average gifts and modest vision.

Sen. Warren B. Rudman (R-N.H.), a close friend, praised Quayle's personal qualities and said he was "vastly underestimated." But Rudman also said he does not think Quayle has the "moral authority . . . the American people are really thinking [about] when they want a president."

"Dan Quayle has a long way to go to be really qualified to be president in terms of leadership qualities," Rudman said, "for a very unfortunate reason not of his doing—and that is the perception with which he is held by the American people."

To many who know him, Quayle seems almost an innocent—and not just because of his youthful good looks and his uncertain speaking style. Unlike many other politicians of his age who have been tested by adversity and tempered by struggles for causes larger than their own careers, Quayle has stayed on the sidelines of the major battles of his generation, and he has never tasted defeat in an important personal endeavor.

Asked why Quayle gives many the impression he has merely "skated on the surface of life," Dan Coats pondered for a moment and then said: "It's possible to grow up and even be a United States senator or vice president, and not really be exposed to, or plunged into, some of the tougher questions of life . . . or brought to the point where you have to make very fundamental decisions about who you are and where you're going."

One thing about Quayle that seems certain, however, is his ambition to be elected president. As one of his closest associates put it, there is "zero doubt" that a 1996 White House campaign is in his plans. There is an aura of political preparation about much of what he does in his vice presidency.

Quayle barely bothers to conceal his goal. Asked directly about his presidential aspirations, he said, "Well, you know what my response is going to be. . . . It's way too early to start talking about 1996. We do early planning to keep options open, and that's certainly an option. Whether we choose to seek that . . . is really down the road."

History is on Quayle's side. Although Bush was the first sitting vice president in 152 years to be elected president, five of the last nine presidents emerged from the No. 2 job through succession or election.

Two sharply contrasting views about Quayle can be heard from people who work daily with the vice president at the heart of the Bush administration.

The case for Quayle is made by Samuel K. Skinner, who, in his new post as White House chief of staff, is in a strategic position to help Quayle achieve his ambition. In a fall 1991 interview, when he was still transportation secretary, Skinner explained why he would be comfortable seeing his golfing buddy succeed Bush.

"Number one," Skinner said, "his basic values are right. Number two, his political judgment is solid. Number three, he is not wrapped up in the trappings of office or those things that would cloud his judgment. And number four, while young . . . he has had an experience that is very significant.

"I have seen no flaws in his judgment process that would lead me to believe that he is not ready to make those [presidential] kinds of decisions," Skinner said. "I also believe he would surround himself with good people, as he has done on his staff."

Even Skinner, however, conceded that Quayle would have to work "to gain the confidence of the American people . . . because of the perception problem" following the 1988 campaign that his three years as vice president have done little to dispel.

Others in the inner councils of the Bush White House are far more skeptical about Quayle's readiness. They said that, although his staffs have been studded with exceptionally bright aides, Quayle's mind is anything but rigorous. They described him as someone who relies on oral briefings, seems to retain little from what he reads and often gives the impression that he is satisfied with a surface brush-by that barely reaches beyond the bumper-sticker level of sophistication.

While his efforts during eight years in the Senate included some examples of concentrated, effective work on job training and defense issues, these Bush administration colleagues noted he has no track record as an executive in developing, launching, sustaining and carrying through to success a complex policy initiative.

In 1988, when Bush surveyed Republican senators, not one of Quayle's colleagues listed him among the top three choices for the vice presidency. One insider has summarized his feelings about Quayle this way: "I think he's smarter and probably more qualified than some people who have been president of the United States in our 200 years. But I think also that if you and I sat down and said, 'Let's each rate the five guys in the Republican Party who are the most qualified to be president of the United States,' I'm not sure Quayle would end up on the list.

"It's tough to make the argument that he is absolutely the smartest and most qualified guy, but at the same time, this airhead stuff is really unfair. He's somewhere in between . . . and he's a hell of a lot closer to the top than he is to the bottom."

PRESIDENTIAL STANDARDS

When Mondale was asked recently how to judge a sitting vice president, he replied that he "has to be measured against the presidency. . . . This is a high standard, admittedly a vague standard, but yet it's the essential standard: Does this person show the depth, breadth, strength, integrity, vision, spirit, the essence of what we would want were he president?"

Like President Bush and most other successful politicians, Quayle is less a man of ideas than he is a tactician who relies on his "people smarts" to gain a competitive edge and achieve his goals. "You do the policy, I'll do the politics," he told Robert M. Guttman when he hired the Library of Congress professional as his top domestic assistant in the Senate.

The Quayle-Guttman partnership produced the piece of legislation that stands as Quayle's most significant achievement as a senator: the Job Training Partnership Act (JTPA) of 1982.

That bill took a largely discredited relic of the Great Society—the Comprehensive Employment and Training Act (CETA)—and replaced it with a private-public partnership that remains, a decade later, the basic program in its field. Although JTPA is criticized for "skimming" the easiest cases, no one has come up with a better idea to replace Quayle's handiwork.

Quayle wrote the JTPA proposal and steered it to passage in his first 20 months as a senator, forging an unusual bipartisan alliance and negotiating or bluffing his way past major roadblocks put up by the White House, the Labor Department and his own committee elders.

"He knew what was a senator's job and what was the staff's job," said Guttman, now a Labor Department official. "He had a feel for the politics and enough understanding of the substance to know whether it was possible. It was an amazing performance for a freshman senator."

That conclusion is endorsed and documented by University of Rochester political scientist Richard F. Fenno in a case study he published on Quayle's Senate work.

"The alliance had survived," Fenno wrote, "because of the mutual trust established between Quayle and [Sen. Edward M.] Kennedy. . . . Quayle's interpersonal skills in carrying out his strategy obviously counted. . . . While he behaved often like an overexuberant kid, he also seemed very much at ease in dealing with fellow senators."

The quality of Quayle's political judgment also wins him respect inside the administration. Both John Sununu and Samuel Skinner have said they relied on Quayle's assessments of the congressional and national scene. Sununu described Quayle as "somebody that we go to for a reality check . . . for a political check, for a substance and policy check." Skinner added, "He can do it in a clinical way, not an emotional way."

By his own testimony and that of staff aides, Quayle absorbs more substantive information through his ears than through his eyes. He attributes that to his 12 years in Congress, "where you probably get more . . . orally, through hearings and briefings," than by reading. He and his aides said he can readily recall what he has heard.

It is not clear, however, how much Quayle extracts from his reading. Several times in the course of interviews for these articles, he mentioned how important conservative British journalist Paul Johnson's book *Modern Times,* a sharp critique of collectivism and the welfare state, had been to him; he said he had reread the first half of it during his August vacation. In a final interview with *The Washington Post,* Quayle was asked what he took away from the book that is "important in the way you look at the world?"

"Well," he said, "I just think that from my strictly historical view of the 20th century, that is probably, that is, you know, the best book I've certainly read. And he goes through it; he starts around the turn of the century up through Vietnam. And it is a very good historical book about history."

Asked what overall concept he had extracted from it, Quayle replied, "Well, I think that the concept, you know—you go through how Hitler, you know, grows to power—sees these types of people that are able to feed on the moment—how he has a huge popular support in Germany at the time. It got into the whole, the arms control aspect, and the decline of the defense posture before World War II.

"He has a very good—and it was something I hadn't thought of, and it's not my area of expertise—and that's how the economic, the international economics, played in all these problems that we had in the 20th century. But there is a rise of these totalitarian leaders. Lenin—a lot of good stuff on Lenin and Stalin."

Aides to whom this is a familiar type of incident suggested that Quayle may have a reading impediment, which could also account for his struggles in delivering speeches from prepared texts. Quayle denied it. "I'm not a speed reader, but I wouldn't say I'm a slow reader. I get through . . . news summaries and things that I've got to get through about as quick as anybody, really," he said.

When told that even close associates suggested that he has a short attention span, Quayle acknowledged that "I've heard people say that. I don't feel that I do, because when I'm interested in something, I'll stay in focus on it as long as is necessary. . . . If you get off on something I'm not very interested in, it's very easy for me to block it out. It's easy for me to block things out."

When Mondale offered Quayle some suggestions on the vice presidency after the 1988 election, he said he stressed one point: "Don't trivialize yourself. . . . You are the heir apparent to the presidency. . . . Stay on the big issues."

Quayle has done that—up to a point. He meets daily with the president when they are both in Washington and is part of virtually all the decision-making meetings. But he does not appear to carry great weight in these discussions.

In what may have been the most crucial domestic policy decision of the past three years, Quayle and his Cabinet allies were unable to persuade Bush to renounce the 1990 budget negotiations led by Sununu and OMB director Darman.

Quayle has let some of his own major initiatives languish while he has tended to the ceremonial busywork of the vice presidency.

The proposals for civil justice reform he launched with great publicity in the summer of 1991 have yet to be translated into concrete legislation. And despite his notable Senate achievement on the issue of job training—and the widely recognized need for coordination of the government's multibillion-dollar training efforts—Quayle acknowledged in a November 1991 interview that "I haven't spent a lot of time on it."

FAMILY, RELIGIOUS VALUES

Many who have watched Quayle said that his principal strengths are the "integrity" and "spirit" that Mondale listed as qualities on which a vice president should be judged. Quayle's values are strongly rooted in his family and his religious faith, and the equanimity of his temperament is mentioned by nearly everyone who knows him.

Dan and Marilyn Quayle are remembered by a former teacher of their children in McLean as "the kind of parents you wish every child had—conscientious and continuously involved in every phase of their life." He coached his two sons' athletic teams, shaping his campaign and Senate schedules around their practice and game times. Even with the hectic schedule of his current job, both parents work hard at maintaining something close to a normal family environment at the vice president's mansion.

Quayle said he was "raised in a Christian home, by a Christian family." At 17, he said, he and friends in a Methodist youth group decided to make "a public testament" to each other of their "personal and emotional attachment to Christ as savior." Quayle described it as less a "born-again" experience than a "maturing and intensification . . . [of] my Christian faith."

Like many others in public life, Quayle argues that there can be no absolute barrier between church and state. "You can't separate ethics from public policy. You can't separate morality and good government," he told a Methodist group in the summer of 1991. "I have to wonder how much better life would be today for millions of Americans, especially women and children left behind in poverty, if our churches had concentrated on personal morality instead of public policy."

The Quayles attend the Fourth Presbyterian Church in Bethesda, which left the mainline Presbyterian Church (U.S.A.) in 1986. Its pastor, the Rev. Robert Norris, said in an interview that he preaches that "a committed Christian has an obligation to be evangelical and outspoken."

"On the positive side," Norris said, "he [Quayle] has produced a good family. His negative is [that] his Christianity is not high-profile. He could encourage Christian work. At that level he is a failure. In some way we are all failures at that."

"I certainly can understand his perspective," Quayle said in response, "and respect it."

Although he has chosen a church with a proselytizing ministry, Quayle emphatically rejects that role for himself. He said he regards his faith as a "very private" matter and is sensitive about "crossing a fine line where you will be criticized . . . for trying to impose your religious values on others. As long as I'm in public life, I'll never do that." Yet religion, he said, is "an important part of [my] everyday life. . . . I don't think there's any time that I have had a challenge that it hasn't helped."

Marilyn Quayle and many of the Quayles' friends suggested that religious faith and a naturally upbeat disposition enabled Quayle to get through the 1988 campaign and the ridicule he has encountered as vice president without any apparent resentment.

The 1988 campaign included "a lot of pain" and "some very dark moments," Quayle said in an interview. But, he added, "I think what I sort of recoil against is [the idea] that the whole vice presidency has been a long, dark journey. That is not a fair description. It's been a wonderful opportunity and a wonderful job and I thoroughly enjoy it."

The face Quayle shows the world is optimistic, friendly and tolerant. Ken Khachigian, the former aide to Presidents Richard M. Nixon and Ronald Reagan who was assigned to Quayle as a speechwriter in the 1988 campaign and remains a friend, remarked, "He's not a natural nutcutter, as Dick Nixon might say. . . . He's like a young Reagan. He doesn't have that dark, moody side Nixon has.

Never once in the entire time I traveled with him did I see him explode . . . in anger or berate a staff member. Not once."

At times during the difficult early days of the 1988 campaign, Quayle appeared to be rattled. But Khachigian said, "If you're looking for somebody who is steady under intense and extraordinary pressure, you've got a man who handles it very, very well. He has a sense of equanimity about him that I find remarkable."

Housing and Urban Development Secretary Jack Kemp, a Quayle rival for the 1988 vice presidential nomination and a potential challenger for the presidential nomination in 1996, agreed. "Quayle is very unassuming, very ego-free for a political leader," he said. "He's not mean-spirited. He doesn't go around dropping poison on people. . . . He doesn't have a mean bone in his body."

Indeed, many remarked, he seems to go out of his way to avoid personal conflicts. Soon after the 1988 election, conservative activist Paul M. Weyrich urged Quayle to emulate Spiro Agnew and pick some fights that would antagonize the liberals and make conservatives say, "This is my guy."

"I must say that I have never been less well received in anything I have ever said to a friend," recalled Weyrich. "He just said, 'Well, I thank you for the advice, but that's not appropriate.' "

"Everyone gets mad and gets frustrated," Quayle said, "[but] there's no reason to really get angry and hateful. I wasn't brought up that way. . . . Angry and vindictive people . . . normally don't get ahead."

Pressed further, he said, "I can get mad but I don't brood about it. I'll tell you what you do is you change the subject," he said, changing the subject.

CONSERVATIVE CREDENTIALS

Quayle is generally perceived as a committed conservative. John Walda, his 1978 opponent for the House, called him a typical "anti-establishment, anti-government, trash-the-bureaucracy type. . . . I really think he was deeply committed to the New Right standards."

But Quayle's conservatism almost always appears tinged with political calculus. Within the family, friends said, he is subjected to semi-serious rebukes for "liberal tendencies" from his father, a former member of the far-right John Birch Society.

Asked what political operator he most respects in the Republican Party, Quayle named former senator Howard H. Baker Jr. of Tennessee. Baker, who led Senate Republicans during Quayle's first four years there, left a reputation as an effective shepherd of a diverse GOP flock. But to many on the right, Baker is a symbol of unforgivable ideological flexibility.

Political scientist Fenno called Quayle an "operational conservative," one whose approach was shaped less by ideology than by his appraisal of the political situation. He worked with Kennedy on JTPA and with Sen. Carl Levin of Michigan, another liberal Democrat, on military procurement reform. Yet Quayle is regarded by leading conservatives as firmly in their camp. He received significant help from New Right organizers such as Weyrich in his first campaign for the House in 1976 and remains close to most leaders of the conservative movement today.

A vital link with the right is his chief of staff, 39-year-old William Kristol, the son of neoconservative authors Irving Kristol and Gertrude Himmelfarb. As well connected to Washington's conservative think tank–political–journalistic network as anyone Quayle could have found, "Kristol brought [Quayle] instant credibility when he badly needed it," according to one right-wing operative outside Quayle's circle.

Throughout his career, Quayle has surrounded himself with aides with exceptional academic credentials. In addition to Kristol, three other PhDs occupy top jobs with the vice president. William J. Gribbin, a history major from Catholic University, a former college teacher, Senate staff member and editor of the last two Republican Party platforms, runs his Capitol office; Karl D. Jackson, an Asia expert with degrees from Princeton's Woodrow Wilson School and MIT and experience at the Pentagon, is on leave from the University of California-Berkeley faculty to serve as Quayle's national security adviser; and Mark J. Albrecht, a veteran of the CIA and the Rand Corporation and former Senate staff member, is executive secretary of the National Space Council.

Fellow lawyers occupy two other key staff jobs: Allan B. Hubbard, a graduate of Vanderbilt and Harvard's law and business schools, is deputy chief of staff and executive director of the Council on Competitiveness. His press secretary, former *Time* magazine correspondent David Beckwith, is a graduate of Carleton College, Columbia University and the University of Texas law school.

Like many of the neoconservatives on his staff and among his outside advisers, Quayle is an ardent defender of Israel. Although he says "the Jewish community in Indiana opposed me very vigorously in 1980," when he challenged incumbent Democrat Birch Bayh, he was a reliable vote for Israel in the Senate and is a favorite among American Jewish organizations—and a target of criticism from State Department Middle East hands.

On cultural issues, foreign policy and defense, Quayle "fits anybody's definition of a classic Republican conservative," as Khachigian said. Kemp described Quayle as an early ally in the fight for tax-cutting, market-oriented economic policies. "Quayle . . . never let orthodoxy stop him from thinking about and exploring new ideas," he said.

Quayle has been counted as an ally by anti-abortion forces from the beginning of his career, but has never made the controversy a centerpiece of his own politics. When Senate Republican leaders urged him to join the Judiciary Committee, Quayle told them he did not want to spend his time wrestling with the social-issue agenda.

Asked about the Supreme Court's *Roe* v. *Wade* decision, which established a constitutional right to abortion, he said recently, "I was never supportive of that decision myself because I think it went a bit far. . . . I would welcome it being overturned . . . but I'm not a judge. My answer is political, not judicial."

He has spoken to anti-abortion rallies in the capital, but in the interview he said, "I think people make a mistake trying to exploit it in the political realm."

Asked how he thought the issue would be resolved, Quayle said he looks forward to the time when "*Roe* v. *Wade* is overturned and it goes back to the states. The states will basically have different laws on when abortion will or will not be allowed."

Asked whether he would be happy with permissive laws in one place and restrictions in another, Quayle said, "I think that's clearly where we're going."

DRAWING TACTICAL LESSONS

Quayle's comment on abortion is indicative of his oddly distant relationship with the great controversies and experiences of his generation. Whether it is abortion, Vietnam, the civil rights movement or Watergate, he has consistently avoided placing himself at the center of the struggle. Sen. Coats said, "I see Dan as someone that really wasn't significantly influenced by those times." If Bush was "selecting somebody to represent that generation, I don't think Dan is representational."

The lessons Quayle draws from the great events of the last two decades are always tactical—never moral. Asked what he learned from the Watergate scandal that led to Nixon's resignation, for example, Quayle said he found it "amazing" that when the cover-up began to fail, Nixon "wouldn't call people in. He didn't know what to do . . . except get mad."

Quayle cited public relations tips rather than warnings about the Constitution and presidential power as the lessons of Watergate. "If there's something you absolutely can't put out, don't put it out. But don't put out something that is factually or materially incorrect. And don't let it dribble out. . . . And once you put the stuff out, don't go having to change your damn story."

On Vietnam, Quayle was a "hawk." He probably has been questioned more often about his decision in 1969 to join the Indiana National Guard rather than risk being drafted than about any other topic. But neither then nor now does he seem to have reflected seriously about the dilemma that Vietnam posed for the nation and for millions of individual citizens—or the way it shattered the previous generation's foreign policy consensus.

Asked what he thought Vietnam did to the country, Quayle said, "It certainly did weaken us [because] around the world we became perceived as impotent." The lesson he drew from the period, he said, was: "State your missions clearly. State your objectives clearly. Make sure you can achieve them, and then achieve them. I mean, it is not much more difficult than that."

Asked about his personal decision, Quayle said: "Look
... I've got the greatest respect for those who served in
Vietnam in combat, but we all make our choices in life, and
I chose to serve in the National Guard and didn't go to
Vietnam. . . . There's no use in going back and saying 'What
if,' or 'I'd rather do it differently.' I have no regrets about
what I did. Given the same circumstances, I'm sure I'd do
the same thing all over again."

The civil rights movement and its repercussions on
American life seemed to have touched Quayle even less
than these other struggles.

His hometown of Huntington, Indiana, had no black
families. As vice president, Quayle operates in an almost
totally white environment. Asked if he had black friends or
black staff members "you regularly consult with," Quayle
said, "Well, Carolyn Washington runs the house, and we
see her every day." Washington is an administrative aide
who manages the stewards at the vice presidential residence and organizes social events held there. She has no
policy responsibilities.

Yet Quayle said, "I am convinced that I can bring people
together," across racial barriers "because I'm committed to
equality and they would know that, and I think they would
see a genuine openness about concerns of others."

Could a President Quayle "bring people together"?
Could he unite and lead Americans from the White
House? Could he even satisfy his own contemporaries that,
in him, they would have a suitable spokesman and leader?

Mondale said he has a certain sympathy for Quayle,

"because the office is handmade for ridicule and for dismissal. In the nature of it, you always look like a supplicant, a beggar, a person on a string."

But in the corporate world where Mondale now operates, he said, "I don't think they see him [Quayle] as a president. I think they think he's light. And most of them I'm talking about are Republicans. I don't think they see strength. I don't think they see power. I don't think they see a person who's moving and shaping his times."

In the final interview for these articles, Quayle seemed to accept Sen. Rudman's judgment that he still lacks the moral authority to be president. "There were probably very few presidents in our history that had the moral authority before they became president," he said, citing three victorious generals—George Washington, Ulysses S. Grant and Dwight D. Eisenhower—as those who did. "Very few others," he said, "had moral authority before they came in.

"You never know until you come to that what kind of a president you can be," Quayle said. "The individual doesn't even know."

So you don't know? he was asked.

"I think, because of my own inner confidence, I think I'd be good at anything I set out to do."

12. Waiting in the Wings for 1996: Organization Takes Shape, but Quayle Has Yet to Prove Himself as a Candidate

Dan Quayle receives a kiss from a well-wisher at an unscheduled stop in a Cleveland mall on a trip in December 1991.

Although Quayle's public speaking remains a problem he has not addressed, he fares better in informal question-and-answer sessions with reporters.

Shortly after Vice President Quayle had spoken at a memorial service for former senator John G. Tower (R-Tex.) in 1991, Quayle's close friend Sen. Warren B. Rudman (R-N.H.) phoned him.

"Dan, do yourself a favor," Rudman recalled saying. "Get a [video] tape of that speech and [look at] the part when you were giving the speech. You were wooden; it was a manufactured Dan Quayle. And then [look at] the part when you departed from the text and told the anecdote. That is the Dan Quayle we know. You'll see the difference."

In a recent interview, however, Quayle said he still had not looked at the tape and, more broadly, acknowledged he has not done much to improve the public speaking problem that media consultant Roger Ailes, among many others, said is probably the biggest barrier to convincing American voters that he should be taken seriously.

He has shown signs of improvement in his television interviews. After watching Quayle's most recent extended network interview, in November 1991 on ABC's "This Week with David Brinkley," an expert in that medium, Dean Kathleen Hall Jamieson of the University of Pennsylvania's Annenberg School of Communications, said it seemed "a perfectly comfortable interview. It didn't make any news, but he looked like a perfectly normal vice president."

But three years after he failed to make the transition from the ad-lib style he had always used in his Indiana campaigns for the House and the Senate to the scripted speeches the Bush campaign insisted he deliver in 1988, Quayle is no closer to solving the public speaking problem. In the six months that *The Washington Post* traveled with him, his speeches repeatedly were marred by inappropriate emphasis on unimportant phrases, by curious inflections and by stumbles. He often looks and sounds as though he is reading the text for the first time. Marilyn Quayle, in an interview, pronounced judgment: "He can't read a speech."

Quayle's staff members said privately that they have urged him in vain to address the problem. Quayle said he is reluctant to bring in speech coaches because of the potential media reaction. "They'd say, 'Boy, he's really trying to get his handlers involved and . . . create this new image,' " he said. Besides, he added, he is too busy to bother with it right now.

So the problem remains unsolved. "That is something I'm going to have to deal with at some time," he said. "I have not dealt with it significantly."

IMAGE PROBLEMS CONTINUE

Quayle's overall image also shows room for improvement. He scored a 50 percent approval rating as vice president in a *Washington Post*–ABC News poll at the beginning of January 1992, with 33 percent saying they disapprove. But when those same people were asked if they think Quayle would be qualified to take over as president if something happened to George Bush, 50 percent said no and 44 percent said yes.

But despite the serious problems Quayle still has to overcome, many of the mechanisms for a 1996 presidential campaign are being put in place.

His hundreds of trips around the country for local and state Republican organizations put Quayle in contact with scores of potential supporters. His political aide, Jim Pitts, a South Carolinian and protégé of the late Lee Atwater, estimated recently that "of the 50 state chairmen, you could probably easily count 10 or 15 fall-on-your-sword Dan Quayle people, probably another 20 who are loyal to [whoever is] the Republican vice president and probably five or six out there who are just going to hate him, no matter what he does." A senior party official who works closely with the state chairmen said Pitts may even be underestimating Quayle's strength.

Senate Minority Leader Robert J. Dole (R-Kan.) said that he concluded from his 1988 campaign for the GOP presidential nomination against then–vice president

George Bush that any vice president—by virtue of the money, staff and spectacle he can bring to a political appearance—would automatically overshadow other contenders. "They've got a lot of advantages," Dole said.

Quayle also has begun to exploit another perk of his office—the vice presidential mansion on Massachusetts Avenue NW—where he and his wife have hosted dinners in honor of Republican governors such as John Engler of Michigan and Carroll A. Campbell Jr. of South Carolina.

It is evident that a national Quayle network is beginning to take form. "Before [1988], there was . . . no following at all," Quayle said. "There's certainly a following now, a hardcore dedicated following. . . . We know who our friends are and who our friends aren't."

It is Pitts's job to nurture that network. He has outlined an agenda of political targets, focusing on battleground states for the Bush-Quayle ticket and "what we see are going to be long-term Quayle support areas—the Midwest, California, the South." Every couple of weeks, Quayle meets with several Republican political consultants to talk about developments in the races they are working and to solicit ideas for his and the president's use.

Some 400 volunteers have been recruited as advance men and women, working occasional gigs for the vice president. Since last fall, Quayle friends have served as co-chairmen of major fund-raisers for the Bush-Quayle ticket, and the vice president expects a similar pattern in state campaign organizations now being set up.

In the 1984 Reagan-Bush campaign, Bush arranged with Reagan's reelection team to be able to pick half the campaign people in the key counties and states. Many of them became his operatives in 1988. Quayle said in interviews that "there's an understanding that the 1992 [Bush-Quayle] campaign will be pretty much along the model of the 1984 [Reagan-Bush] campaign."

Quayle aides are also collecting names of political allies he can assist in finding jobs in a second Bush administration, strengthening a cadre that today is very small. Success in that endeavor could strengthen his hand against such potential 1996 GOP rivals as James A. Baker III, who already has several supporters in key jobs.

DIVIDENDS IN THE BUSINESS COMMUNITY

Quayle's work as vice president has also brought some political gains. His anti-regulatory zeal as chairman of the President's Council on Competitiveness has endeared him to business executives who are actual and potential campaign fund-raisers. Much of business also joins the broad public applause for the attack on the "excessive" cost and burden of litigation that Quayle launched in a speech to the American Bar Association (ABA) convention in Atlanta in August 1991.

When Quayle's speech drew an immediate rebuttal from ABA president John J. Curtin Jr., the vice president enjoyed a rare flurry of favorable media attention.

Beyond providing Quayle his first opportunity to go toe-to-toe with a political antagonist since his ill-fated 1988 debate with Democratic vice presidential nominee Sen. Lloyd Bentsen (Tex.), Curtin gave the story an element of personal conflict that put it on the television news and the nation's front pages. Editorial writers rallied to Quayle's side and he was, at least briefly, exultant. But Ailes dismissed the whole episode as "a blip on the screen" and said in a recent interview that the audience that really matters for Quayle is the one that will watch his acceptance speech at the convention in August 1992 and his debate with the Democratic vice presidential nominee.

Some of Quayle's foreign travels have helped his political prospects at home as well. In August 1991, Quayle and Secretary of Commerce Robert A. Mosbacher led a trade delegation to four nations in Latin America, accompanied by the chief executives of nine major American banks and businesses.

These men—most of whom had had little prior exposure to Quayle—came back singing his praises. David Rockefeller, the dean of the group and veteran Latin American hand, commented toward the end of the trip that Quayle's unscripted response to a dinner toast by Argentine president Carlos Saul Menem was "as warm and gracious a statement as I can ever remember hearing an American official make down here."

"I've found Quayle's statements throughout the trip to be knowledgeable, friendly and appropriate," said Rockefeller, the former head of the Chase Manhattan Bank. "If anyone had come on this trip without knowing his past image, you would think the United States could not be better represented."

Like Rockefeller, William T. Esrey, the chairman of US Sprint and its parent, United Telecommunications Inc., had heard Quayle two years ago at a meeting of the Bilderberg Group, a blue-ribbon international business organization. Like Rockefeller, he had thought Quayle's performance then so stiff and scripted that "he should not have been sent" to represent the Bush administration. On this trip, by contrast, Esrey said he was impressed. "In the meetings we've had with him, he establishes rapport very quickly, gets right to the issues and gets agreement."

"This group will spread the word," said Donald B. Marron, chairman of PaineWebber Inc. "We've talked among ourselves, and I think everyone was really impressed. All these things you hear about him don't match up to the reality."

STUCK WITH FIRST IMPRESSIONS

But one does not have to dig very far into the conservative network to find doubts about Quayle's presidential strength, when measured against such potential rivals as Baker, Jack Kemp, Richard B. Cheney, Sen. Phil Gramm of

Texas and, doubtless, others. Heritage Foundation's Burton Yale Pines, an admirer of Quayle and his staff, said recently, "I'm not sure Quayle ever recovered" from the damage of the 1988 campaign. "The firestorm literally traumatized the guy. . . . First impressions are important. It takes a massive amount to change them. And I think he's stuck with his."

Gary L. Bauer, president of the Family Research Council, said the ridicule of Quayle cuts both ways. "There are a lot of conservatives who will like you solely because you've been criticized in *The Washington Post* and *New York Times*. On the other hand, that constant level of criticism probably causes some conservatives to wonder if he would be a viable candidate for the White House, I mean, a horse they could bet on."

Paul M. Weyrich, president of the Free Congress Foundation and a mentor of Quayle's in his first race for Congress, said in the fall of 1991 that in the early speculation for 1996 among conservative Republicans, Quayle "is not in bad shape, but he's not in good shape. I travel a great deal across the country, and when we discuss the 1996 situation, his name almost never comes up. I have to bring it up. And when I bring it up, people say, 'Well, you know, maybe by then he'll prove himself.'

"But right now, he doesn't have much of a following out here. . . . He's gone out and campaigned for a lot of people. . . . Surprisingly, he is the second-biggest draw that the party has. . . . He's considered a plus if he goes in and raises money. But people at this point are not thinking of him in terms of the presidential standard-bearer."

Whether Quayle can get pols—and voters—to think of him as a presidential standard-bearer will depend in large part on the impression he makes in the 1992 campaign. He has campaigned around the country trying to limit support for columnist Patrick J. Buchanan's anti-Bush effort. "The next real opportunity for the American people to get a good glimpse of me will be the 1992 campaign," Quayle said recently. The fall especially "will be a very important 2 1/2 months."

As if to spur his efforts, Quayle has surrounded himself with reminders of the vast distance between the vice presidency and the presidency. On the walls of his office just off the Senate floor are portraits of Schuyler Colfax, Thomas A. Hendricks, Charles W. Fairbanks and Thomas R. Marshall, the four Hoosiers who preceded him in the vice presidency. All of them were presidents of the Senate. Not one became president of the United States.

Photo Credits